BJ 1012 .C315 2000

Capitan, William H.

The ethical navigator

G. ALLEN FLEECE LIBRARY
Columbia International University
7435 Monticello Road
Columbia, SC 29203

THE ETHICAL NAVIGATOR

William H. Capitan

University Press of America, Inc.
Lanham • New York • Oxford

LP653   172

Copyright © 2000 by
University Press of America, ® Inc.
4720 Boston Way
Lanham, Maryland 20706

12 Hid's Copse Rd.
Cumnor Hill, Oxford OX2 9JJ

All rights reserved
Printed in the United States of America
British Library Cataloging in Publication Information Available

Library of Congress Cataloging-in-Publication Data

Capitan, William H.
The ethical navigator / William H. Capitan.
p. cm.
Includes bibliographical references and index.
1. Ethics. I. Title.
BJ1012.C315   2000   170—dc21   00-036446 CIP

ISBN 0-7618-1700-X (pbk: alk. ppr.)

⊖™ The paper used in this publication meets the minimum
requirements of American National Standard for Information
Sciences—Permanence of Paper for Printed Library Materials,
ANSI Z39.48—1984

For my Mother

She taught me the difference between right and wrong.
When I was six, she saw I had a toy airplane we didn't
buy. She took me by the ear, walked me the better part
of a city block into the dime store where I had stolen it,
up the stairs to the manager's office, to return the toy
and apologize for my offense.

Contents

Preface

This book results from my unique encounter with students at the University of Georgia. After a long run as a university president, I thought I had enough of disputes among persons over race and politics, legal battles, government regulations, and religion to last me for the rest of my life. Then I had the good fortune to teach in the Honors Program at Georgia. When I entered the classroom after more than twenty-five years as an academic administrator, I was not sure I would be able to teach very well. Indeed, things were different.

The students were just as bright, but I soon learned that if I wanted to communicate with them, I would have to find new images and new examples, not from classical literature but from television, film, science fiction, and newspaper headlines. More importantly, I was amazed by how the students tolerated differences in personal values, how little they let on if anyone said something I regarded as shocking about personal conduct, and how skillful they were at managing the ambiguities this tolerance created. I marvelled at the complex world they saw themselves preparing to negotiate.

Still, I thought I saw something in their faces when I was able to present philosophical arguments for traditional morality, parts of it at least. And the religious ones in the class seemed to sit up just a little when they detected the possibility their beliefs about right and wrong may even be rationally defensible. Everyone seemed surprised to learn there were ways of addressing right and wrong outside the Supreme Court, the Congress, the headlines, and popular appeal without resorting to blind religious fundamentalism. In short, almost every one of them was surprised by ethics.

That is why I have written this book. If these very bright young people destined, beyond doubt, to become our leaders had so very much to learn about morality, what about all the others in the successor generation? What about their predecessors who either forgot to teach them morality or found it insignificant? I hope this book will stimulate interest in the moral life, create discussion of matters moral, carry us beyond the talk show hand wringing about moral decay, and even, once again, make morality a matter of public discourse.

I thank all of the gifted, charming, young people so filled with ambition and promise for listening to me and encouraging me. Above all, I thank them for their patience as the clock ticked past my philosophical elaborations. My debt to R. G. Collingwood will be obvious. Philosophical errors, great and small are mine alone.

In addition, I thank Mildred Tietjen, my long time colleague in administration, for editorial assistance, Ann Cacoullos for suggestions to improve the manuscript, and Dolores Capitan for helping me through intricate thoughts and words.

*****

"The Second Coming" (first stanza) Reprinted with the permission of Scribner, a Division of Simon and Schuster from **The Collected Poems of W. B. Yeats**, Revised Second Edition edited by Richard H. Finneran. Copyright (c) 1924 by Macmillan Publishing Company, renewed 1952 by Bertha Georgie Yeats.

"Law Like Love" (selected lines) From W. H. Auden: **Collected Poems** by W. H. Auden, edited by Edward Mendelson. Coypright (c) 1940 and renewed 1968 by W. H. Auden. Reprinted by permission of Random House, Inc.

"Mrs. Robinson" (selected lyrics) Copyright (c) 1968 Paul Simon. Used by permission of the Publisher: Paul Simon Music

Introduction: Who's In Command?

People throughout the ages have lived and worked together for their mutual advantage. Civilization itself began as individuals worked together to advance common interests. Individuals are able to work together by knowing what to expect from one another and then relying on one another to say and do what their life together requires. While life may be possible at arms length from one another, individuals of candor, honesty, and trust believe life shared with others is better than life alone. Morality makes that possible.

Today many people think of morality, not as the fabric of their society, but as the remnant of bygone days holding them to old ways of doing things and old ways of thinking. For them morality is something they do not need, a restriction on their freedom. They think people should be free to live their own lives and they should let others live theirs. They think people should be understanding of one another. They try to live by their own religion or their own personal values. They go along to get along with family and friends and leave law and order to others, to government and the courts, perhaps.

There is something attractive about this way of thinking. No one wants to be known as a busy body meddling in other people's lives. If we want to be free, we have to leave others alone. If we want our privacy, we have to keep our noses out of other people's affairs. This thinking is commendable in many ways. It is, nevertheless, fundamentally erroneous. It overlooks the cooperation required for individual freedom. It overlooks the fundamental element of morality: one's freedom exists only because others help secure it.

We each assure our own freedom by behaving in ways that assure the freedom of others and they do the same for each of us. That, of course, is not a one time thing. We can each remain free only if we keep acting in the right ways. I cannot lay down my arms and let down my guard unless I know you will, too. But I can really do this only if I can be sure everyone else will continue doing so. This requires more than an understanding: it requires a relationship of trust. This is the foundation of morality and the essential element of civilization. It secures our freedom allowing us to explore the possibilities for our lives and to work together to realize them.

Morality has had a complex historical development, and it has pervaded civilized life. We have each lived as a part of it. Until now, we have always assumed that a moral authority of some sort controlled us. We have had theories about what or who keeps it going. We have thought it was a god, or a priest, or a minister, or a king, or a judge. Even though these authorities may have been at odds from time to time, we have always acted as though someone was in charge of our moral lives. We have not stopped to consider that maybe it is we ourselves who have been keeping it going by acting civilly toward one another.

In the present era anyone claiming moral authority is beset by others claiming moral authority and they in turn by others. Questions and answers about how people ought to live come from a variety of sources—doctors, lawyers, elected officials, religious ministers, athletes, and media personalities. They seem to be talking about the same thing, and yet they do not come to the same conclusions. The questions and answers are often inconsistent because they are raised and lowered in different contexts.

Sometimes these are *bona fide* moral questions, and sometimes they are not. Sometimes these so-called moral authorities are seeking moral answers, and sometimes they are not. Very often they are people with specific agendas masquerading as morally concerned but in reality interested in going their own way without any regard for morality or the rest of society. Sometimes they are the reverse. They masquerade as objective scientists, reporters, or jurists without moral inclination interested only in revealing to us how things really are. In fact, they are presenting moral points of view quite at odds with the moral requirements of the society.

This lack of moral consistency creates the adverse living environment we are experiencing today. No society trying to live with it is viable. Morality requires our expectation that all adult members of the society participate fully. It will not work with a few people expected to behave morally and everyone else not. Morality cannot be floated unless everyone is expected to share in the effort. But people, especially young people, who have never seen morality operate and have never been taught its worth, cannot be expected to help keep the ship afloat. They need to see what morality means to them. Then they may consider making sacrifices required to support a fully functioning morality. This requires isolating morality from life for a philosophical instant to see what it is and how it works.

The moral chaos we face today results from three mistakes. The first is failing to recognize civilized life rests on the reasonable expectation that everyone in a given society will interact positively with one another. The second is thinking people can live and work together without sharing the same beliefs about how they ought to behave toward one another. The third is substituting religion, government, law, science, or mere custom for morality. This is not to say these have no bearing on morality, nor even to say that morality is not substantially related to them. But it is to say these often displace morality and lead us unwittingly into moral confusions resulting in ruinous actions and a debilitated society.

This book provides the necessary overview of what morality is and how it is different from and at the same time related to religion, law, government, and custom. The following chapters distinguish morality from what are commonly thought to be morality but are actually morality substitutes. They then show how the life reasonable people desire requires the positive interaction of individuals in the responsible relationships traditionally known as morality.

This book is a manual for people who recognize error in living as if morality does not matter or even if it did matter, they can do nothing about the present amoral way of life. It shows how morality has worked and is supposed to work. It shows why choosing to live morally is reasonable and why ignoring the moral dimension of life is not. It shows how we can once again chart a moral course.

We must learn to navigate morally in the sea of human affairs. We cannot expect to sail through life safely free of those who oppress us, free of those who refuse to honor our freedom, until we can see how to set our course. We will not be captains of our own moral destiny until we assert ourselves together as the one true moral authority.

Chapter I

ℰↄ◌ℛ

Who Needs Ethics? Moral Drift

Turning and turning in the widening gyre
The falcon cannot hear the falconer;
Things fall apart; the center cannot hold
Mere anarchy is loosed upon the world,
The blood-dimmed tide is loosed, and everywhere
The ceremony of innocence is drowned;
And the best lack all conviction, while the worst
Are full of passionate intensity
—W.B. Yeats, "The Second Coming"

"Save the world again, James? For England."

"For England, Alec."

And so the daring 006 and 007 did in the first scene of Goldeneye.[1] Later in the film we learn 006 has brutally betrayed his fellow agent, Bond, and England. Coming out of the movie mist, 006 or Alec Trevelyan says: "Hello, James. Back from the dead. No longer just an anonymous star in a memorial bulletin at MI 6. What's the matter, James? No glib remark, no pithy comeback?"

"Why?"

"Hilarious question, particularly from you. Did you ever ask why? Why we toppled all those dictators, undermined all those regimes? Only to come home . . . 'Well done, good job, but sorry, old boy, everything you risked your life and limb for has changed'."

"It was the job we were chosen for . . ."

"Of course, you would say that. James Bond, Her Majesty's loyal terrier, defender of the so-called faith . . ."

"Yes, I trusted you, Alec."

"Trust. What a quaint idea. . . .

In our time known for its moral decline, it is at least interesting that an immensely popular film would turn on matters of loyalty, patriotism, and principle. Alec and James are mortal foes because one betrayed friendship and country and the other trusted and remained true to his commitment. We are meant to admire the steadfast Bond and to detest the wily Trevelyan. Bond is honorable, sworn to defend the nation, to put duty before self, even sacrifice his life, friends, and his own memorial, if need be.

Do these values still beat in our hearts? Patriotism has taken some hard knocks, and even the Bond film characters have a slightly cynical tone when they say "for England." This doesn't show during the playing of the national anthems at the Olympics, though. Is that because we can enjoy being patriotic for as long as it takes to sing the national anthem? Do we cling to our other values as entertainment, to feel good from time to time, even though we believe it naive to risk real advantage for their sake, not to mention life and limb?

Bond, despite his seeming weakness for beautiful women, appears to use even the beautiful Natalia for the sake of the mission. When she is used as a shield by Bond's foes, Bond tells his foe to kill her, "She means nothing to me." Later, Natalia assails Bond's ultimate value, doing his sworn duty:

"He was a friend, Trevelyan, and now he is your enemy and you will kill him."

"In a word," says Bond, "Yes."

"Unless he kills you first. . . . Do you think I'm impressed? How can you act like this?"

"It's what keeps me alive."

"No, its what keeps you alone."

While much of this is movie dialogue to be dismissed as just that, it implies Natalia's perception that there is more to life than a given mission. This is countered by what we are supposed to find admirable in Bond, his sense of duty. In this scene his all consuming sense of duty is apparently held at the expense of human sentiment.

Here is the fundamental ethical question of our time: can we allow moral duty to interfere with desire—kindness, love, understanding, acceptance, caring? What of these values so touted in modern "culture"— movies, television, and magazines?" Are these the right ones? Is Natalia right in offering love and condemning Bond's plan to kill his enemy for the sake of duty. Wouldn't loving your enemy be better than killing your enemy? Is acting from love better than acting from duty? This is how modern "culture" sees it: the really good people act from love and the stuffy, overrighteous act from duty.

With every fiber of his being 006 tries to do what is expected of him only to be told it really didn't matter, "that was then and this is now." Maybe the objectives of society are misguided, or, as implied here, ephemeral. Maybe the only way to deal with this is to go one's own way. The cold secret agents frequently experience is commonly understood. Less well understood is the cold we ourselves experience when we try to do the right thing only to be made out in the eyes of others, or even our own, as fools.

So does it come down to every one for one's self? Is this being selfishness or just being smart in today's world? Maybe it's not just the world today. Maybe it has always been that way. These questions are not new and they have not been ignored by moralists over the years. But they do seem to be more pressing today. And the answers seem more elusive. Where do we turn for answers? Why try to be moral? How do we live the moral life even if we choose it? What is morality? Who is our moral authority? Religion? Whose? The United States Supreme Court?

Never before have we had so much ethics—business ethics, medical ethics, conduct codes, ethics committees, preachers, and pundits. The 1996 Presidential Election, many claimed, was about values, particularly, family values. The debates never clarified whose values and what a family was. And are matters of family to be decided by governments, anyway?

Many writers would be our moral authority. Most of the really difficult ethical questions that wrestle us seem personal. All the ethical questions we face—divorce, suicide, adultery, sexuality, honesty—seem like matters of personal choice. Are they? If not personal choices, for whom then? Is someone else going to tell us what we are supposed to do? Is it the courts? Who knows really why court cases come out the way they do? It is our duty to obey the law. Right? Duty, again.

People believe the nation's moral foundations are crumbling. Many hope to re-establish them, some by return to what they believe were the moral foundations, others by their particular views of right and wrong. And they want to do this at a time when our understanding of the world and what is in it is being radically revised by scientific discoveries, amazing technological transformations, almost unimaginable medical procedures, and prospects soon of more we cannot even imagine now. Think of how our moral views of marriage or of crime have changed in the last fifty years because of psychology alone.

It is no wonder modernists consider moral rules as the butt ends of old folkways in place long before we knew about human sexuality, sociology, and all the rest we now know. Isn't it time we freed ourselves from the bondage of ethics, whatever that means in today's world? If people really use the knowledge they have about human behavior, they will "understand" and "accept" others and especially themselves. After all, isn't that loving and forgiving our neighbor?

Yet, this modernist attitude toward human conduct, dominant in recent decades, may have a considerable social cost. A battle has emerged between personal freedom and social responsibility. Our physical well being has improved. Our inhibitions have been lowered. We are not so frustrated. Most of us have the things we want, and there is much more for us if we go for it. The same can hardly be said about our social well-being. Owning that BMW is glorious, but worrying about the altogether too real prospect it will be stolen is agony and trying to get it back when it is stolen is hell. Going to a fine restaurant gives a great sense of physical well being, but looking over your shoulder in the restaurant parking lot to and from your car fearing for your life does not.

"Things are bound to get better. Right?" To answer that, take a look at the social well-being of the coming generation. Adolescent homicides and suicides have risen dramatically in the last few years. The rates are still rising. Much of this violence takes place in schools where we are used to the prevalence of theft and cheating. Out-of-wedlock births (only please be reminded that the politically correct term is "nontraditional births") now account for approximately 30% of the total number of annual births. "These are problems affecting minorities and poor. Right?"

Wrong. These social ills are affecting all income groups and both blacks and whites.[2] Illegitimate births are rising fastest among white middle class teens. Crime is increasing among youths in very affluent neighborhoods, too. One reason offered recently for the rapid rise in illegitimate births has been the lack of commitment to marry in case of a pregnancy. It used to be the "honorable" thing for men to do and a precondition to consent to sexual intercourse for unmarried women. But why should one bother to get married? Why should one bother to use birth control measures? Why bother even to get an abortion? One recent solution by a young unmarried privileged couple was to go a motel, birth their baby, and then murder it.[3]

There has been a marked resistance to taking responsibility for one's actions. We have found ways to blame "factors" beyond our control, someone else, and when that doesn't work, to diffuse responsibility through use of the passive voice: "Mistakes were made." We have designed programs, provided counselors, given courses in every day living, including sex education. We are even giving courses in moral education. This social breakdown in families, schools, and practically all of our institutions affects us all. Business, industry, marriage, government, the military cannot long endure without honest and responsible people. Who wants a doctor or an airline pilot who cannot be trusted? Who is responsible for unwanted babies and unwanted family members? Who pays and what is the cost?

How did things come to this? When was the last time you heard anyone say unequivocally that something is immoral? Why is that so difficult to do? Did we, somehow undetected, all stop doing the right thing, or have we gradually forgotten how to tell the difference between right and wrong? Maybe there never was a difference between right and wrong, and we are just now realizing it. There are many reasons. Most people would agree, though, that science has profoundly affected our sense of right and wrong. We have found scientific explanations for many natural phenomena, and we are confident those phenomena we cannot explain now we soon can. In particular, we can explain a great deal about the behavior of people, as individuals and as groups. Knowing how people in fact behave tends to vitiate ideas about how they ought to behave.

For example, we know that there is going to be a certain amount of shoplifting in our store. We will, to be sure, take counter measures, but we know there is a point where the counter measures will cost more than the shoplifters. Being "realistic" we simply plan our business around the anticipated shoplifting losses, raise our prices to cover the losses, or even bear the losses to avoid annoying buyers not wanting to shop with guards or electronic equipment creating an unpleasant "siege" atmosphere in the store.

Also, looking for the payoff leads people to cheat, lie, and steal in the many ways available to them in modern life—insurance claims, travel reimbursements, quarterly reports, and government forms. We know all that paperwork isn't checked carefully, and being caught is unlikely. When changing a few statistics on a quarterly report will make no difference to the decisions the company makes but will make you look good at the board meeting, why not do it? We know that is what people do. Why put yourself at a disadvantage by being "literal" about things?

The more we know, the harder it is to think about right and wrong. We know the sex drive of teenagers is awesome. They are going to have sex. "It's natural." How can we say it is wrong? We have data on the infidelity of married persons, on the rate of divorce, on the extent of promiscuity of almost any category of people you can imagine. We know what people do. What ought they to do? The moderns argue against traditional morality by using scientifically gathered information on what actual practice is in contrast to what anyone might say it should be. If we had been raised the way the people in a certain economic, social, or ethnic group were, then we would act the way they do, too. How can we say which ways of which groups are the right ways? Some philosophers have put it this way: one cannot derive an "ought" from an "is."

Movies and television for years have sought to delight viewers by showing what's hot and what's cool. Moralists and media critics have accused these media of promoting radical departures from traditional moral practices, often to the surprise of the media who see themselves as merely recounting what is. After all, if a certain subject or its treatment does not please viewers, the media are not likely to present it. But as it is presented, it tends to change attitudes among those for whom the subject or practice presented is new. It is very hard to find a black and white film from the forties that is not filled with cigarette smoke, or one from the sixties that is not filled with sexual promiscuity. These presentations may not cause people to behave as the actors, but a film or television show by including such behavior could imply approval. Moreover, it does it without being subject to the standards of rational criticism and canons of social viability.

The point here is not so much to critique the media as to show how depiction and documentation of certain behaviors displace notions of right and wrong. Walker Percy provides a slam dunk example in his *Lost in the Cosmos*.[4] A young woman writes to Dear Abbey for advice. She finds the cost of birth control pills is becoming burdensome. She thinks her boyfriend should share this expense because, after all, he is benefiting, too. Her question is this: Does she dare ask him to share the cost of the pills when she doesn't know him well enough to talk about money? This is serious business—a boy and girl matter of extreme delicacy, to be sure. But a great many questions of right and wrong evaporate in the press of such practical matters.

It is difficult to think about right and wrong because we do it only on rare occasions, when circumstances conspire to force us. By and large we see ourselves as going about our business meeting our needs in the practical world using what science and technology tell us about how to get what we want. If we do not feel good, we find a pill to make us better. If we are mentally upset, we seek a pill for that, too, or, if need be, go to a therapist to get fixed. We see ourselves basically as physical. Our thoughts, feelings, and desires we direct primarily toward our well being as we understand it in the natural world. A major shift in the way we understand ourselves has happened. We have become part of the natural world.

The moral dimension of our self-understanding is gone. We now view ourselves mainly as animal creatures acting out our destinies, albeit with a bigger brain. Our hopes and aspirations, our desires, our views of what ought to be, become so many natural facts. What you think ought to be done in a given situation may not be what I think ought to be done. We have different views, but the fact is, our views are merely our opinions. In this way matters of moral judgment appear to us as subjective, "personal," but mainly not to be disputed because, concerning anything other than matters of fact, there is no sensible way to argue for our own views other than to communicate how we feel.

Moral talk has virtually disappeared from our discourse. We have substituted psychological, sociological, legal, and political language for it. When someone behaves badly, messes up his life spending too much time away from his work doing things we used to call immoral such as fornicating, we handle that by saying he is "immature," or, possibly, that he has "psychological problems." When a person is given to stealing, and nowadays it has to be much stealing, and this results in a "problem" for that person and possibly others, we refer to that as "antisocial behavior." We are hardly going to call it "wrong," illegal, maybe, but hardly wrong. Given our understanding of the social factors involved, such as that person's having grown up in a rough neighborhood, we "understand" and do not condemn. To do so would be to make a "value judgment." Educated people are supposed to know better. They are "open minded," not "judgmental."

There is another reason it is hard to call acts right or wrong. This is not new in history, but, as with all historical recurrences in our century, it is magnified because travel and communication are so fast. Contact with other cultures, and the high degree of diversity even within nations presses us to think and be multicultural in our thoughts and deeds. It presses us to be "nonjudgmental" in our interactions with people from different cultures. Who are we to tell people from other countries or even from different parts of our own country what to do, and who are they to tell us? A kind of relativism enters our thinking, and, without any real way to decide who is right or wrong, we acquiesce in seeing what comes out in the wash. We live and let live.

When we learn of practices among other peoples conflicting with what we consider right, it may lead us to examine what we consider right in that regard and even to modify our views. Euthanasia is a complex subject, and its moral approval or disapproval is affected by many considerations. When we learn it is legal in Japan and the Netherlands, we wonder if the predominant moral attitude in our society is the one we should have.

Closer to us personally are differences on moral matters among people we see at parties and at work every day of different religious or ethnic backgrounds or just different moral beliefs. Maybe you decided not to make a fuss when your daughter of a certain age came home with her live in male companion and the two of them expected to share her bedroom. Maybe you decided that because you wanted to "keep peace" in the family. Then who are you to look down on the children of others you are sure are sleeping with their boy and girl friends? Better to keep your mouth shut lest you be called a hypocrite. Right? Those other kids may be younger than your daughter, but who knows what "old enough" is these days?

If you are at lunch with your good friend and she tells you she is pregnant but just can't go through with it because this is "not a good time" and she is having an abortion Friday, do you risk getting ugly about it and insisting on your ideas about abortion when that is really "her business?" After all, you don't want her telling you what to do with "your body," do you? You know she is already very upset. You are not going to be "judgmental" because you don't know really for sure what you would do in the same situation. Why ruin a good friendship? You are not in charge of right and wrong for the society, and what society, anyway? She goes to a different church and lives in another part of town.

Many forces seem to wrest moral control from us, moral control so hard to assert in the best of times under the best of circumstances, hard enough for ourselves, let alone for others. Yet the essence of morality lies exactly where we say we can't operate: in the voluntary interaction of individuals. The moral dimension of life appears when people freely choose to work together for a common purpose. When these conditions are present, we have a society as opposed to a mere cluster of people, and only when we have a society in a real sense do we have morality. Morality requires voluntary association for a common purpose. Without voluntary association and common purpose, we cannot "expect" anything of others unless we plan to force them into doing what we expect of them. The same goes for others' expectations of us.[5]

Since the association is voluntary, everyone in the society is equal: no one has more authority over the other than each is willing to give to the other. Here is a hint of how independence and equality balance. Each is independent because each voluntarily chooses the association, and each is equal to the other because any power over others assigned to any by the society is assigned for the sake of attaining the common purpose of the association.

This is the foundation of morality. There is much more to be explained about morality—how it works and how we decide what is right and wrong, but unless a moral community exists, as a "society" as opposed to a mere collection of human beings, we can be neither moral nor make moral judgments. It is because we have omitted this fundamental element of morality in our thinking that we are living in our moral quandaries today.

Who is our neighbor? Who is our brother, our sister? Indeed, who is our father and who is our mother? Who is our child and who has custody of it? Mobility, upward and downward, drive by and sleep over, state, local, and national. Where do I fit in, and with whom am I in voluntary association? How can I tell? These are difficult questions, and they must be answered, but it is one certainty that without a society, there is no morality and without morality there is no society. There is only what we are seeing in the world today: the brink of social chaos.

It is necessary to begin somewhere, and this is where I have chosen to begin. It is also necessary to make assumptions. Ultimate principles do not admit of proof in the usual sense of that term, whether they are principles of science or of morality. The truth of what follows lies in what it explains about morality and whether it shows us a reasonable way to live and how to tell the difference between right and wrong. We could stop to argue at any point, but we risk becoming mired in scholar's technicalities. This is what led Nietzsche to say, "I have departed from the house of the scholars and the door I have also slammed behind me. Too long did my soul sit hungry at their table."[6]

We risk fragmenting our real questions and answers about morality. There is no substitute for careful reasoning, but we do not have the scholastics' luxury of time for endless debate. I choose to avoid the kind of scene drawn by Dickens. Substitute "moralist" where Dickens uses "advocate." It goes as follows:

> . . . some score of members ought to be—as here they are—mistily engaged in one of the the ten thousand stages of an endless cause, tripping one another up on slippery precedents, groping knee-deep in technicalities, running their goat-hair and horsehair warded heads against walls of words and making a pretense of equity with serious faces, as players might.[7]

We do not have the advocate's luxury of pretense. Ours is an urgent and sincere quest on behalf of a society on the verge of moral collapse.

Notes

1. *GOLDENEYE*© Danjaq, LLC and United Artist Corporation. All rights reserved.
2. *Kiplinger Washington Newsletter,* June 2, 1995.
3. For a gripping story of two privileged people who do just that see Doug Mast, *Always in Our Hearts: The Story of Amy Grossberg, Brian Peterson, and the Baby They Didn't Want,* Record Books, 1999.
4. Walker Percy, *Lost in the Cosmos,* New York, The Noonday Press, 1992, p. 43.
5. R. G. Collingwood, *The New Leviathan,* New York, Oxford University Press, 1959, pp. 132ff.
6. Friedrich Nietzsche, *Thus Spake Zarathustra,* Part II, XXXVIII.—Scholars, Willard Huntington Wright (ed.), *The Philosophy of Nietzsche,* Random House, New York, 1940, p. 135.
7. Charles Dickens, *Bleak House*, New York, New American Library, 1980, p. 18.

Chapter II

୫୦୯ଌ

What is Ethics? Reckoning with the Good Samaritan

". . . every community is established with a view to some good"
—Aristotle, *Politics,* Book I

Moral life begins when two or more individuals are joined for common purpose, each individual freely enters or acquiesces in the common purpose, and each is free to act as a rational adult. The individuals are equal because each partakes equally in the common purpose, its rights, privileges, and responsibilities. In a moral society, anyone who has any more of these than anyone else has them because it furthers the common purpose and so the others willingly give them to him. Anyone who has any less of these than anyone else has less by virtue of not participating fully in the common purpose or by virtue of not being a rational adult. The individuals are free because they are voluntarily bound to the common purpose. They are equal because they share equally in the common purpose, its benefits and its responsibilities. Failure to consider these fundamental requirements has led to the moral confusion we experience in our time. Unless all of these elements are present, there can be no morality.

Contemporary discussions of right and wrong center on individuals—individual rights, individual freedom, and individual equality as if these exist apart from relationships among individuals. A right, as commonly understood in modern societies, is a power or privilege to which a person has a just claim. But the claim is against other persons. For the claim to mean anything, it must be acknowledged by the other persons, either because of an accepted agreement or law or custom. Otherwise the one who claims the right has to secure it by force.

Now why should others acknowledge a claim of rights? Because they see acknowledgment of that right as contributing to the life they all are trying to live together, in other words, their common purpose. Without common purpose a group of individuals is merely a collection of humans who happen to be born in the same place or otherwise arrive there. This is not a society because here no one knows what to expect. One does not know what is expected of him and can expect nothing of others because they don't know what is expected of them either. In such a place, who has what rights, what freedom, and what does it mean to be equal? That will depend upon what, if anything, they understand themselves to be doing there together.

The history of individual freedom is often recorded as people wresting back their rights from their sovereign. Some political philosophers have spoken as if isolated individual humans laden with their own individual rights came together to form a union and in doing so gave some, but not all, of their individual rights to the sovereign. According to these philosophers, individuals gave up some of their "natural rights" to obtain from government certain "civil rights." But the actual historical development of rights has been quite the opposite: liberty, the freedom of the individual, exists, not in a state of nature, but in human society with an already existing purpose recognized by each individual as common to all.

Being free is being free from dominance by the forces of nature and from force of a person or class of persons more powerful or "more important" than we the people are. Freedom results from working with one another rather than against one another to surmount natural threats and disasters and exploiting the possibilities of life. The history of revolutions against tyranny is the history of socialized humans freeing themselves of interference in their lives. Without the overbearing force of the tyrant the people are free to live their lives together, only now without interference from "the authorities."

Ignoring these facts has led to the positing rights as auras hovering about the heads of individuals or fetched from thin air. Rights posited in this manner can be multiplied seemingly on demand. Such ignorance makes it all too possible to think of free individuals as possessing vast quantities of rights and all too impossible to think of free individuals as owing any moral responsibilities to one another. But without responsibilities to one another, as we have seen, we can make very little sense of rights. Without relationships born of shared purpose, there can be no rights. And without rights there can be no freedom.

Equality is best understood as another view of individual freedom. Most of us are familiar with the beliefs, slogans, and historical documents on equality—children of God; universal brotherhood; "liberty, equality, fraternity"; "we hold these truths to be self-evident: that all men are created equal and are endowed by their creator with certain unalienable rights." What is self-evident? It was once self-evident that monarchs ruled us by the right given them by God. And while we may all be "children of God," it was not clear until two centuries after the Declaration of Independence that women should have the right to vote in America, and later still that African Americans should. We could say we are just now getting around to interpreting those phrases. But, if that is so, then what guides us in our interpretation? Surely the drafters of the Declaration of Independence had a different interpretation when they used the phrase.

The fathers of the American Revolution believed we are created equal because, among other things, we share in reason, at least white males do. But that was long before Darwin, a time when humans were thought to share in the divine by being possessed of reason, formed in the image of God and the angels. In contrast, today humans are seen as quite other than partakers in the divine. They are part of the very natural order of animals, supremely intelligent, but still animals; and rational at times, but also capable of anger, fear, and rage; altruistic at times, but also largely selfish, normally self-centered, and, more often than not, carried away by emotion and desire. All people are not equally endowed with reason, some being far more rational than others, some far more intelligent than others. Humans are unequal in a great variety of ways—strength, cunning, physical beauty, motivation, and acuity of perception, not to mention wealth and privilege.

Then, what are we really saying when we say that we are equal? We are saying something like this: "let it be that we are equal," or "each person in our society shall count for one." We say that each person is equal before the law. We know this is not really so; some people can't afford the lawyers other people can. But we say it anyway. Most of the time we are saying it as a principle we intend to follow. Sure, it's not really like that, but we will try as hard as we can to make things work as if everyone were really equal. "If you cannot afford an attorney, we will appoint one for you." Never mind that this attorney is fresh out of law school or available for your defense for want of a high paying client. But why should we even try to do that? Why do we pretend and not face the scientific facts about equality?

People who think they can base ethics on facts usually try to do so even when the facts don't fit with their ethical expectations. For example, equity feminists are those who hold that women are equal to men in all respects. We should just drop the trappings of traditional male dominated culture. When equity feminists encounter certain facts inconsistent with their ethical claim of sexual equality, they seem studiously to avoid the facts. I have in mind some findings of evolutionary psychology indicating differences between the ways men and women think.[1]

We must allow for culturally instilled differences because humans as a species are malleable and culture usually defines sex roles strictly. But, even when we do, we find sexual behavior does not lead comfortably to the conclusion that the sexes will naturally behave fairly according to social expectation. The male in most species of mammals, not all, but most, does the sexual pursuing and the female the sexual attracting. The male tends to be promiscuous and the female not. So, not only are men bigger and stronger physically than women on average, but by nature men can't even be expected to act like women when it comes to sexual fairness and fidelity. Anyone expecting males to treat females as equals will have to find something other than nature as a basis for that expectation.

What puts us in a position to expect equal treatment from others is social not natural. What are we really saying when we say that we are equal? We are saying something like this: "let it be that we are equal," or "each person in our society shall count for one." If we are going to work together as a group to accomplish something, we are going to have to expect certain things from one another in full measure of cooperation. If my personal freedom is at stake, I can help assure not having it taken away from me by helping assure it is not taken away from others. If we are going to expect full cooperation from everyone, then everyone will have to benefit equally from that purpose. We are not going to have special classes of people, not intentionally. Just what all we share, whether it is equal opportunity or mutual protection or the fall grain harvest, depends on the life we work out together. We try to make facts of individual differences irrelevant to individual liberty and social equality.

The business we have together allows us to make claims against one another. But what is this business we have together? The story for the Good Samaritan gives a hint. An expert on the laws of Moses asks Jesus, "What does a man need to do to live forever in heaven?" Jesus asks him, "What does the law of Moses say about it?" And the man replies, "It says that you must love the Lord your God with all your heart, and with all your soul, and with all your strength, and with all your mind. And you must love your neighbor just as much as you love yourself." Then Jesus says, "Right. Do this and you shall live." But the man wanted to justify his lack of love for some kinds of people and so asks, "Which neighbors?" Jesus replies with the story:

> A man going on a trip from Jerusalem to Jericho was attacked by bandits. They stripped him of his clothes and money and beat him up and left him lying half dead beside the road. By chance a Jewish priest came along; and when he saw the man lying there, he crossed to the other side of the road and passed him by. A Jewish Temple-assistant did the same thing; he, too, left him lying there. But a despised Samaritan came along, and when he saw him, he felt deep pity. Kneeling beside him the Samaritan soothed his wounds with medicine and bandaged them. Then he put the man on his donkey and walked along beside him till they came to an inn, where he nursed him through the night.
>
> The next day he handed the innkeeper two twenty-dollar bills and told him to take care of the man. "If his bill runs higher than that," I'll pay the difference the next time I am here."

After telling this, Jesus asked, "Now which of these three would you say was a neighbor to the bandits' victim?" And the man replies, "The one who showed him some pity."[2] In other words, the one who saw that the plight of the victim was something that concerned him is the neighbor.

That the Jews and the Samaritans despised each other leads us to conclude that Jesus means being a neighbor ought to be understood broadly, and that makes a valuable Sunday School lesson. The story is also telling us we ought to feel compassion for our fellow humans. But there is much, much more being said, and it takes us to the heart of ethics. To grasp the central meaning, we have to look at its entire context—answering what is the fundamental duty according to Mosaic Law. The story is not just about compassion, but about our duty to fellow human beings. Compassion helps, and maybe without it we can't sense our duty to others. But the point of duty is usually missed because there is so much else in the story.

It is also missed because of the tradition of interpreting the ethics of Jesus as sorrow for the sufferings of the weak. This led Nietzsche to declaim Judeo-Christian ethics a slave morality saying that, "only the poor, the powerless, are good; only the suffering, sick, and ugly, truly blessed."[3] This tradition of interpretation may be reinforced by movie and media morality whose ultimate criterion of value is whether a scene expresses deep personal feelings. But none of this is the essential meaning of the story.

Notice the word "pity" used in this context: the true neighbor, despised though he was because of the prejudice against Samaritans, was "the one who showed him some pity." This word is not a synonym for either compassion or empathy; rather, it is a word derived from "piety" referring to devotion to religious duties and practices. We can't just love somebody on command. God can command it because it is, not a feeling or an emotion, but a duty to act toward others as you would have them act toward you. The good Samaritan was performing his duty to love his neighbor as himself, to do for him what he himself would have wanted done had he been in need. That is what it means to love your neighbor as yourself, not what Nietzsche imagined it to be—to love your neighbor and not yourself. The commandment is to recognize the responsibility toward the victim because in this fortuitous life the Samaritan and the victim really are equal: they are born, suffer, and die.

The other two passersby did not recognize they and the victim were neighbors. What happened to the victim could happen to them, and for all of the contingencies in life, they are in it together. They have the same needs as the victim. This is what they have in common, and this is what makes them equal. Things like this can and do happen to any and all of us. We depend on others to help us and they depend on us. Compassion comes upon us because we recognize this similarity among us, not the other way around. The passersby may even have empathized, but, without recognizing they are bound together by their common condition and equal nature, they would see no obligation to do anything, and they didn't.

As for Nietzsche, he got it wrong. I confess that I, myself, used to wonder what was so special about the poor and downtrodden to Jesus. I now realize that his interest may have been because in the poor we see more keenly what it means to love our neighbor as ourselves. The poor are the most vulnerable in any society and the rich are the least vulnerable. But rich or poor is not what determines equality. What does is recognition that the needs of others are just like ours, and if we care about ourselves, we should care about others. The basis of morality is mutual protection against life's risks and misfortunes. We relate to one another morally when we act in light of these risks and misfortunes.

This is obvious in how we care for one another in our families. It is less obvious, but no less true, when we extend this relationship beyond family and beyond others we obviously need and who need us. If we were victims of bandits, we would want someone to help us, whether family, friend, or stranger. Also, there does not seem to be any special reason our needs should be met and not the needs of others. After all, we are all neighbors because we share the need for security against the misfortunes of life. That is why Jesus taught that we have a duty to love our neighbors as ourselves. That is the meaning of equality, and that explains why we refuse to let scientific facts interfere, even when there are clearly discernible material differences among us. We try to act in ways that regard each and all of us equal.

It has always seemed a particular piece of sentimentality that idealists who get religion typically feel they have to go and serve the poor. True, the poor and widows and orphans have great need, but, unless there is also recognition of the needs of the rich and famous, Christianity and most of the major religions become common social doctrines bent on solving material inequities, and hardly the means to spiritual enlightenment. I remember a minister who worked for a Christian organization as a fund raiser. He said his ministry was to the rich, to provide them an opportunity to give of their wealth to help the poor and perhaps pass more easily through the eye of the needle and into heaven. Even with the intended humor, his point is still valid: Christians have moral duties toward the rich, too, because from the moral point of view the rich are equal to the poor.

The rich have various means at their disposal when they are beset with difficulties. If they lose the roof over their heads, they can replace it through insurance or money from bank reserves or loans. The poor are against reality with no options and their suffering as humans is conspicuous, just as a rich man's is when he is suffering from an incurable disease no amount of money can cure, and just as all of us are in our mere mortality. In this way we are all equal, though it always takes a great moral teacher to remind us. Incidentally, the story of the Good Samaritan does not indicate the economic status of the victim, probably because it is morally irrelevant.

In making our approach to equality so vital to ethics, I have drawn upon Christian scriptures. Here I am not concerned to argue for or against a religious foundation for ethics. It is often interesting and sometimes instructive when a religious teaching squares with a rational conclusion about ethics, in this case the sense of equality. Are we equal because God commands us to treat each other as equals or because we really are? And does God command us to treat each other as equals just because He wants to or because we really are? Plato, in his dialogue "Euthyphro" asks a similar question, Is a moral commandment what we ought to do just because God commands it or because the commandment is right? Why would God command us to treat one another as neighbors? It seems sufficient for God to command each of us to work out our own relationship with him, to find our destiny on our own. What have neighbors to do with this?

Let's look again at the good Samaritan. He is the very same person who comes upon the man fallen among thieves and lying bleeding and helpless. Only this time suppose this same good Samaritan does not stop to help. Is he still the good Samaritan? He is the very same person who did stop, only he didn't stop. Well, we have to say we just have no way of telling. But the good Samaritan knows. Doesn't he? How does he know? Maybe he knows he would stop if he could, but this particular time he is in a hurry to get to his business. He could say he knows he would because he believes it is the right thing for anybody to do. But under what circumstances? When it is less trouble? When it is no trouble? The point is even we ourselves cannot know our own character unless we really act. Would God even know what is really in a person's heart until the person determines it through making an actual moral choice? But there is more.

Accepting the obligation of mutual assistance is also rejecting mutual harm. Each of us gains freedom from others and reduces the threats of misfortune. The individual who chooses to act morally becomes liberated from both external and internal constraints—reducing the force from tyrants and fellow humans and from the fortunes of life. And choosing to act morally is choosing to control and direct one's actions for his own security freeing oneself from emotions that impede self-direction. As this happens one becomes conscious of his freedom; he recognizes it in others, and others recognize it in him. The spirit of freedom we trace through political history as freedom from domination by others is paralleled by a growth in consciousness of individual freedom as control over ourselves by ourselves.[4]

This is not, as many moderns would have us believe, the caprice to do anything we please, a kind of Nike shoes commercial sense of freedom. Progress toward personal freedom is not all that matters, and, indeed, cannot be made by seeking it alone. This is not really freedom because it is not control over ourselves; it is actually the absence of will manifesting itself in weakness. The free individual has the strength to make choices that promote and preserve his freedom, and, as we have seen, that includes protecting the freedom of others. That is moral choice, and making moral choices is the business we have together. Together we become free, and becoming free we increase the options life has to offer each of us.

The interdependence our own equality and that of others with whom we are morally bound will become clearer in the subsequent chapters. Lest we get ahead of ourselves, be reminded that a great deal has to happen in a community of people before full individual freedom obtains.

Here we have the three fundamental elements of morality: equal individuals, voluntarily united, for a common purpose. It is now time to put flesh and bones on these three elements to see how they determine what is right and what is wrong.

Notes

1. See, for example, Robert Wright, "Feminists, Meet Mr. Darwin," *The New Republic,* November 28, 1994.
2. Luke 10 : 25-37 NIV.
3. Friedrich Nietsche, *The Birth of Tragedy and the Genealogy of Morals*, trans. Francis Golffing, Copyright 1956 by Doubleday, a division of Bantam Doubleday Dell Publishing Group, Inc.
4. R. G. Collingwood, "Rule-making and Rule-breaking," sermon preached in St. Mary the Virgin, Oxford, 5 May 1935, Collingwood MS, DEP I p. 10.

Chapter III

෩෨

Right and Wrong: Reading the Chart

"Would you tell me, please, which way I ought to go from here?"
"That depends a good deal on where you want to get to," says the cat.
"I don't much care where . . .," said Alice.
"Then it doesn't much matter which way you go," says the cat.
—Lewis Carroll, *Alice in Wonderland*

Section 1. Individual Freedom and Social Purpose

In a society, as opposed to a mere collection of human beings, each person has cast his lot with the others. This creates a context of security and growth for everyone. According to Aristotle it is our nature to develop our powers to meet our natural needs and to satisfy our highest curiosity, even respond to the awe of existence itself.[1] Each of us can do this only in the supporting context of others. Modern ethical discussions, preoccupied with individual rights, typically ignore our essential social nature. As testament to this we seem only lately to have rediscovered that child nurture is best in two parent families, worse in one parent families, and terrible in no parent families.[2] Think of what it would be like with no society.

To be an individual is to have freedom and the will to exercise it, but as humans we do this most fully in the supportive context of others. Each of us has individual desires, but much of what we each desire is shaped by the common life of our society. In any society there are settled ways of meeting individual needs. Ideally our society will enable each of us to choose for ourselves what we want to have and do with minimal interference and maximal cooperation from others. That makes it easier than trying to go it alone.

But each of us cannot be free and equal and always be in mutual support. Humans beings, even friends, will come into conflict from time to time. Patterns of expected behavior develop to coordinate behavior and minimize conflict. These constitute the morality of the society. Through time, new facts, conditions, and situations emerge stressing morality, requiring us to reflect and find ways to accommodate these emergences. This reflection is called ethics. The purpose of ethics is to study ways to maximize our fulfillment and preserve the social order and reduce the conflicts bound to arise as we do. Because morality is to keep us in rapport with others in our society, morality cannot be "personal" as people are so fond of saying today. If our morality were personal, it would not be much good in defining patterns of cooperation and resolving interpersonal conflicts.

Recognizing our common interest brings home our need to maintain mutual support, even in times of conflict. If we do not recognize our interdependence, we miss the foundation of morality. Those with whom we come into conflict become obstacles for us to circumvent or destroy. We would risk losing one another as we each sought unbridled our individual objectives. We have been involved with one another as we have engaged with nature in the process of living and the refinement of that process—development of higher goals and pursuit of them. This comes first. Ethics comes second when we reflect on preserving our mutual dependence.

Not realizing this order has us so confused in the present day. We try to resolve moral matters by pure ethical reflection without considering the moral foundation of our common life. Just as we are in the society of others for what they can do for us, others are in our society for what we can do for them. No one individual's interest is superior to anyone else's. But it is not as if we have entered into a relationship we can call ethical; it is, rather that we started together on the path toward civilization. We are related to those who raised us, protected us, and transmitted the essential knowledge of the culture so we can be free of fear, fend for ourselves, and effectively fulfill our desires. We have depended on our parents and teachers and those who fought our wars.

Moral life rests on support from our predecessors and current society members. We safeguard this relationship because we recognize that our freedom depends upon it. Here is where the moral bond is found. We experience it among friends. When we grasp it, how consciously I cannot say, then how we should act toward one another is not difficult to discover. We give and receive freely what we need to and from one another. Moral education is for those who do not know how to act toward one another standing in this relationship. That is when we begin talking about how we "ought" to act toward one another. This is not really mysterious. Most of us know what it is like to act out of friendship and to benefit from acts of friendship.

Some members of the community do not appreciate the culture and those who produce, transmit, and maintain it. What, then, of the prospect of their being moral and members of the moral community? This sense is essential for discovering what it is to act morally toward one another. Children do not readily act morally toward one another, and babies are the ultimate self-centered beings. That is why moral education in the form of cultural appreciation is a vital part of every moral society. In recent decades civilization is considered an impediment to freedom. But realizing how we have wrested our lives from hostile others, from ignorance, and from menacing nature is moral understanding. This is hardly encouraged in modern societies, and we are reaping the result in moral decay.

We have been looking in the wrong places for a way to restore morality. We have passed laws. We have opened ourselves to other cultures to avoid being ethnocentric. All of the laws we have passed and all of the conduct codes for business, for this branch of government and that, this profession and that, are trying to put Humpty Dumpty together again. It is impossible to start with every individual as perfectly independent and free to engage in the civilized company of people with no expectations of anyone doing what is necessary to maintain civilization A law is only effective if it rests on a moral foundation. Looking at other cultures as morally equivalent to ours makes it difficult to sense our interpersonal dependence. We can have little regard for this in other cultures unless we have it in our own.

Trying to understand how we should conduct ourselves in the abstract is impossible because, regarding the interaction of humans and their environment, the possibilities are enormous. It is impossible to pull down rules of conduct from pure science or pure reason. A simple story of cross cultural experience will illustrate the point. Edward T. Hall remarks that "the rules governing behavior and structure of one's own cultural system can be discovered only in a specific context or real-life situation.[3] He had to decipher an unusual pattern of behavior in a small country in the Far East where the members of the U.S. official missions were the only Americans in the country.

> On official visits, the Americans were kept waiting inordinately long. It was almost as though they weren't there. Some waited for hours. Even the newly appointed U.S. ambassador was kept waiting! In ordinary diplomatic circumstances such treatment would constitute an official insult to our government. Yet something told the Americans that this might not be the case; there were too many cues to the contrary. Besides, relations between the two countries were friendly and there was no reason to insult everyone indiscriminately, even before the first meeting. The Americans were mystified, of course. . . .[4]

> I eventually was able to identify a pattern that explained the puzzling behavior of their hosts. The Americans were kept waiting because they were not known and had not taken on substance. A newly arrived official in someone's outer office was like an undeveloped film; there was no tangible experiential image of the man. No one knew him as a friend or human being. You could see him and hear him bellowing about being kept waiting and how important he was, but in terms of relationships in a social system he was at best a shadow and one that didn't look too promising at that. Americans who were willing to come back repeatedly and to meet their hosts socially outside the office had a chance to become flesh-and-blood, active members in a social system. Ultimately, they had no trouble being ushered into offices. Americans saw people in terms of their status, whereas the hosts saw them in a larger frame that took more time to integrate.[5]

Hall provides a great deal of analysis in preparation for this conclusion. To be fair to him, he explains at some length the differences between the two clashing cultures. But all we need see is that there is such a fabric and what has not been woven into it has only a shadowy existence. Taking on flesh-and-blood existence in this way is entering the morality.

It emerges when one considers himself and is considered part of the society. But, one thinks, "Anyone would have realized this is not how one treats strangers, let alone diplomats, and this is a matter merely of protocol." Perhaps, but that is not the point: this really happened and we have an explanation for why it did happen.

The American and European paradigm of diplomatic courtesy may be widespread, but it is evidently not universal. That the officials in the small Asian country did not follow it provides an opportunity to observe that cultural fabric is a fact. Later I shall try to show how the limitations imposed by culture can be transcended in a kind of rational ethic, but even that cannot be done unless we first recognize some sense of social purpose accepted and shared by everyone involved. We have here a glimpse of what it means for people of different outlooks to begin to relate to one another morally. The parable of the Good Samaritan is about this, too.

We tend to impose our cultural paradigms upon others as if everyone else's paradigms must be sacrificed in favor of ours. The usual strategy is to make those of others conform to ours and try to destroy any of theirs that do not fit with ours. The human cost of this throughout history has been enormous. Consider the Western European impositions upon the peoples of central and eastern Europe, and upon the peoples of the Near East and in lands seized by the colonial powers. Equally arrogant is the delusion that all societies are morally equivalent and that apparent differences are either irrelevant or immaterial conventions.

Later it will be our task to unravel this erroneous thinking as we move toward finding an objective approach to ethics. Here we have to recognize the cultural bonding that holds every society worthy of the name together. They are the relationships we have to those who help us become what we are, help us in time of need, and provide us the rich inheritance of our present civilization with all of its benefits and protections against the viscissitudes of nature and happenstance existence. To look for the foundation of morality is to look into nothing less than the nature of civilization itself.

In contrast, Thomas Hobbes, the seventeenth century British political theorist presented a picture of pre-social humans as living a life that is "nasty, stale, brutish, and short." Sooner or later, they each catch on that life could be a lot better if they could agree on certain things, set up laws as ground rules for getting along, and establish a central authority to see that each person does what he is supposed to do.[6]

This is an oversimplification of Hobbes' theory, and it is even questionable how literally Hobbes himself took this idea of actually getting together at some point in time to set up a society. Something like the formation of a "social contract" has formed, probably over a long period of time, as humans moved from barbarity to civilization and tried to formalize the resulting relationships among individuals. But the common error in the "social contract" is ignoring everything antecedent to "agreeing" on a social contract. In reality our working relationships with other humans are highly evolved and exceedingly complex.

Another error in social contract thinking is its unquestioned leap to a an all powerful government, the sole source of moral authority by virtue of being the enforcer. The social contract theory is no doubt helpful to political theorists, but it is heavy handed for dealing with morality and the weighty matter of moral reclamation. It makes all societies versions of the modern European state. But there are many societies that do not in the least resemble European or American states. Some societies do not have an all powerful governmental ruler and enforcer of morality. Some ethnic groups have nothing at all like a government as we understand it.

As cooperation developed in the process of each of us meeting our individual needs, so did a relationship of trust and confidence in others in our company. This is the thread to follow in discovering how we move from mere group life to civilized society. We were able to get to the Hobbes social contract stage, if we ever did, when and only when, our relationships of trust were such that we could form a contract.[7] It does not pay to do business with people when you always have to rely on the contract, not unless you want to spend most of your life in a courtroom. It is far better to work with people with whom you have an "understanding" and who have an "understanding" with you. Trust is the glue that holds civilized society together.

In response to threats from the natural world, the challenges of staying alive, and the desire for "fulfillment" in the rich sense of that word, we progressed from barbarism to civilization. Things for many of us became easier, and we have generally forgotten that we arrived by relying on one another and sharing what we know to transcend the natural barriers to a full life. How exactly we got here is the subject of anthropologists and historians. That we got here is a fact. Whether we can remain here has yet to be determined. There is no guarantee that a people, once civilized, will not become barbarians; nor that barbarians cannot become civilized.

We are, from time to time, rudely awakened to our mutual dependence by what insurance companies call "acts of God." Neighbors who rarely speak to one another become closer after a flood, hurricane, tornado, or blizzard. People we never imagined existed come to our rescue, and we help other people. We are grateful to the doctor who saves us or a loved one from a dreaded illness, even though we have for years resented his high fees. The lawyer who sees that justice is done when we are wrongly accused or uncivilly used is a welcomed guest after the trial. We needed her and could not have prevailed without her. Probably the greatest trust is among soldiers and sailors who depend on one another for their very lives.

There are numerous other contexts where we are reminded of the nature of civil relationships. Think of how it feels to find yourself in an unfamiliar part of a large city, hoping to God your car doesn't stop running. Contrast that with your sense of security at home with your friends and relatives. You know how they are going to treat you and how you are going to treat them. You know when they are not treating you the way they should, and you usually know when you are not treating them the way you should. Because we have been so far removed from the raw side of life and only now and then are reminded of it, we forget our need for one another in the course of living our lives.

Civilization is the process whereby humans achieve the freedom that makes life possible. To understand morality we must "schematize" humans as they actually struggle with nature and interact with others to live— with their needs, desires, inadequacies, and fears. Among their needs are procreation, longevity, security, and the promulgation of the knowledge required to succeed in meeting the challenges of nature and to assure the future of the successor generation.

We need easy cooperation between people in rapport. We need to be open with one another, to transmit information useful to one another, and to cooperate for the development of each individual. We need to expect cooperation and not interference from others. As desiring, willing, acting beings, we want to go about our business without others interfering with us and we them. As it has actually happened, we have developed civilization by helping one another.

The relationship of pursuing this common purpose requires moral interaction among the individuals so united. This relationship may be more or less understood among the members of the civilized group, but it must be understood to some degree by everyone who is a full-fledged member. Morality constitutes all of the ways individuals must interact to maintain the condition of civilized pursuits as they are identified and sought by the members. Morality requires us to behave toward one another in ways that assure the flow of vital information. It also requires us to act in ways that build the cooperation we need together to promote, preserve, and protect life.

Aldous Huxley once remarked that "Most human beings have an almost infinite capacity for taking things for granted." After Kent State University was closed following the shooting of students on the Kent State campus, Kent in Exile came to Oberlin to bring their version of the counterculture. The established society was not at all to their liking and they were "dropping out." Things in society weren't going well enough to suit them, so they just were not going to participate. They were going to drive their fast cars to Oberlin, use electricity from the local power outlets, eat food from the restaurants and supermarkets, rely on the local hospital in case of emergency, but they were not going to participate.

That form of parasitism might even be defended as necessary for the social welfare as a form of protest. Though the counterculture people did not, they could have tried to shut down the hospital, poison the water supply, and thwart essential social services. They did talk about such things. As it happened, they were responsible, even so, for the closing of a number of colleges and universities throughout the country. That was not without its social cost. But the point is not to revisit the old clash of values between the counterculture and the "establishment." It is to illustrate that certain behavior is intolerable in an operating society, and certain other behavior is essential. When one does the former or thwarts the latter, we call that conduct wrong. Certain behavior has to be interdicted and certain other behavior demanded in any functioning society, depending on what the members of that society have set about doing.

Every society must have its members do some acts and not do others. The realities the members face and how they understand them determine this. Every group of people faces some of the same realities. Their "response" to these realities shapes their social purpose. The particular response of the society is shared by each member of the society and this generates social consciousness. This is being aware one is a member and choosing to continue as a member. This is being a partner with the other society members and being willing to carry such responsibilities as that may entail. Just as business partners share the benefits of the partnership, they also share its losses. This is particularly significant when one of the partners does not continue to perform. That is why societies have a way of helping those who have fallen through illness or some other misfortune.

Membership in the society is a matter of free choice. The counterculture people chose not to participate. In their case, by their actions and also by what they said, they elected not to share in the duties of society, but they benefited from the advantages and continued to benefit from them anyway. Again, some might argue that protest in an open society is not only to be tolerated, but also necessary for the health of the society. But protest is one thing and dropping out is quite another.

Section 2. Social Purpose and Individual Achievement

A moral community, what I call a society, governs itself. It cannot be otherwise. Its members are adults freely choosing to work together. It rules itself by its members willing to do what it befalls them to do. The moral person does what is right even though not made to do it—wants to further the social purpose and wants others to do so, too. In the United States we have become so preoccupied with government and law we tend to expect no one will do anything for others unless compelled. That makes moral recovery difficult: who tells us what to do? "If it's not against the law, it's moral." I shall examine this error later. Here notice that until we each accept the responsibility of doing what we are supposed to do without force, there is no morality.

There are other ways to pursue one's goals, and most of them have been tried in the course of human events. Most notably various forms of domination have been tried. Despots have made others obey them through coercion. But this has never been easy for either master or slave, and social organizations based on dominance sooner or later fail. Everyone wants to be one's own master whether capable of it or not. People do not like being made to do things they do not want to do. To avoid the resentment people must consent to what they are expected to do. This results in a community of people acting together of their own free will.

The desire to dominate is regularly met with the desire not to be dominated. This is why freedom is central in political history and has become our ultimate value. We have forgotten it is secured through joint effort. Political theorists like Hobbes and Locke even premised their theories on a primordial state of nature in which everyone was "free" and possessed of certain unalienable rights some of which were traded for the security of the state. This may have been a convenient fiction for theorists of the eighteenth century looking to justify revolution against tyranny. But it has led to substantial confusion about rights as indicated by the phrase "human rights" as if one has rights just by virtue of being human.

There is a strangely persistent superstition in modern thought that human beings are entitled to certain things owed us by nature or our fellow humans. Among these are "life," "liberty," and "happiness." But we now know enough about nature to know it is not like that. Nature recognizes no more right to life in humans than in animals in the jungle. Earthquakes, floods, famines and tornadoes recognize no property rights and no rights to food, shelter, or happiness. And our fellow humans, in a measure as they remain "natural" creatures without relating to us in some civilized way, do not either. Because of the vicissitudes of life we are compelled to relate to other humans to create as much stability for ourselves as possible. It is in this relationship that rights and responsibilities are born.

We have so much focused on rights pulled from thin air that we have detached moral questions from their foundation and, as a result, rendered the questions incapable of resolution. Consider as an illustration the matter of human abortion. It should come as no surprise that we cannot reach a consensus on the issue of abortion in American society. We have adopted the freedom of the individual as the starting point of the discussion and omitted what civilized existence requires of us regarding procreation. So the argument for abortion focuses on the right of the pregnant woman to choose whether she wants to continue her pregnancy or not and on whether the fetus has any right to life. Questions about the rights of the fetus center on when the fetus becomes a human being. The rights of others who may be concerned about the pregnancy and the interest of the state are limited to issues pertaining to the health and safety of the mother and the fetus.

We cannot debate abortion as a moral matter because we have made it a question, not about what we need to do about procreation, but about freedom to do what one wants unencumbered by the interests of others. This may be out of despair of ever reaching moral consensus. But if so, when and where was the effort to reach moral consensus ever made to agree on what we expect of ourselves in support of procreation? The matter of rights is relevant, but the main issue is what to do about people making choices that bear on our securing the successor generation. The only way we can have a successor generation is by very careful attention to the unborn, whatever they are, humans or not.

Does one woman's action to abort her pregnancy have all that much import? To ask a moral question is to ask, What bearing does my action have on the lives of people whose common purpose I share? This is how we begin to address the question. This is so for the right-to-life people as well as for the pro-choice people, and this is how they could be in dialogue on the subject. Neither side is asking the right question. The question is, What do we expect of one another in support of procreation?

The right-to-lifers claim the fetus is human and should not, therefore, be killed. The pro-choicers claim the fetus is either not human or has no rights, or at any rate, rights equal to the mother's right of privacy. But the only rights any one has are those that make our life together worthwhile in the pursuit of the goals we share. Whenever we interfere with acknowledged social purpose, our rights can be and usually are abridged. In fact, the only way we have of balancing rights of individuals in conflict is by reference to social purpose

To resolve their conflict, the opposing sides have to determine what they share regarding childbirth. Historically, the sides have developed outside the moral context, in the forum of politics and law. The argument proceeded along the line of individual rights, the right to privacy, the right to control of one's own body. Setting aside constitutional questions about such rights and turning directly to the moral question, what are the consequences of abortion for the society? What implications does having an abortion have for the rest of us, even if it is legal? Is it nobody's business but the pregnant woman's? What about the male parent, the would-be grandparents, aunt and uncles, and what about the successor generation we as a society have formed to protect and expect to protect us?

We can hear the response: "I feel for them, but it is my decision because it is my body." But this merely begs the question: "My own interest in this matter is more important than any interest others may have or think they have." But this is not a moral response. One has to care about the effects of one's actions on others in order to be moral, that is, participate as a member of society. Here lies the moral dimension. Without looking here we cannot expect to solve our moral quandaries or even to understand them.

The "missing" moral content is what we as a society are sweeping under political, legal, and medical rugs. How this works is illustrated in an unusual lawsuit Alan Dershowitz analyzes, an unusual lawsuit both in the nature of the issue and the analysis. The suit is between an estranged couple over seven fertilized eggs, termed a "custody dispute" by the media. Dershowitz hits pay dirt, perhaps without realizing it, as he writes:

> Mary Sue Davis, whose eggs were extricated from her body and fertilized, wants them implanted back in her body so that she can have a baby. Her estranged husband, Junior Lewis Davis, whose sperm was used to fertilize her eggs, wants them destroyed. . . . In the context of a fertilized egg outside the body of the mother, there should be a presumption in favor of creating life, provided that one of the genetic parents is willing and able to provide for the child. If a genetic father wants the eggs to be born—and if he had a willing carrier—then his wishes should prevail over those of a genetic mother who wanted the eggs destroyed. In this case, since the genetic mother favors birth, her wishes should prevail. . . .
>
> Law, morality, and even religion will have to adapt to the new realities, as they already have to other technological innovations that have helped infertile couples. . . .
>
> In resolving the very real dispute between the Davises, the courts should avoid abstractions such as when "life begins," whose "property" the eggs really are, and whether they should be "labeled 'preborn children'." Instead, the courts should look to the practical consequences of their decisions on the real interests of the parties involved. . . .
>
> The donee's interest in producing a child should prevail. The courts should turn the fertilized eggs over to Mrs. Davis so that she can implant them into her body and try to give birth.[8]

Dershowitz says there should be a presumption in favor of creating life. Why? Because that is what Dershowitz thinks about matters reproductive. And that is what he thinks will "make sense" to his readers, and, of course, like much of what Dershowitz says, it does. But it should not pass as anything other than a moral premise in his reasoning. Most importantly, it illustrates how moral disputes cannot be resolved without importing something like this into the reasoning process. It is his attempt to articulate what we share, our moral purpose, in a living, working context, what we will acknowledge as the heart of matters reproductive. Morality deals in nothing other than the practical decisions on the real interests of those involved.

Dershowitz says religion, morality, and law have to think in terms of practical interests, while he reveals no awareness that he is relying on morality in producing his decision on what is right in this case. But he himself brings forth a moral premise, and it is our presumption in favor of life, a value shared by normal human beings. In trying to go beyond "popular opinion," he may just have come upon a moral principle. And why not? The protection of life, in this case as procreation, is and has been a matter of fundamental concern for all societies throughout the ages. It is curious that we have to be reminded of this in a most roundabout way. Modern civilization has so diminished the threat of no offspring we have forgotten how precious birth is to any society. One reason humans live in societies is to protect both the offspring and the elders whom the offspring will protect when they mature.

To be capable of rational solution, ethical issues must be explicated in terms of humans acting jointly toward goals. This is not something we can observe as scientists. We have to look deep into the hearts and minds of the people having the dispute and grasp the goals they share. Sometimes people will think there are goals at stake when there may not be, as in the debate over the practice of homosexuality. One reason people cannot agree about the moral acceptance of homosexual practices is they believe such practices are detrimental to important cultural goals. Underlying the goals of various societies are common biological and psychological needs among all humans. Also, there are organizational requirements for meeting the needs. Do homosexual practices interfere, and can the conflicts be resolved either by the adjustment of the practices or modification of goals with which the practices are presumed to conflict?

It is tempting to jump to the conclusion that if we could just list the goals all people recognize, we could then develop a universal set of ethical principles for all humans and begin holding ourselves accountable to them. This may not be possible, but if it is, it will not be simple. There are some encouraging indications in modern anthropology to suggest it could be.[9] It is reasonable to suppose there are underlying common biological and psychological needs shared by all humans, and if this is so it is equally reasonable to suppose there are some individual and some social goals common in all societies.[10] It is also reasonable to suppose only certain social structures will be adequate to allow the members of any society to meet their goals.

But it is also possible some goals of the various human cultures may be mutually incompatible. We may not even be able to eliminate conflicts from a culturally complex population such as that of the United States. This is for later consideration under the subject of ethical relativism. For now, all we need recognize is that there is a rational process whereby ethical disputes can be addressed within societies, and it will proceed along the lines indicated in the Dershowitz example. This is because ethics reflects on goal directed activity requiring concerted action by the members of the moral community. It requires individuals, committed to a common purpose with regard, at least, to the matter at issue.[11]

The individuals must be freely committed to the purpose, that is, voluntarily. If they are not, one or more of them will be to that extent enslaved to the other, and, of course, if not committed freely, then there is no basis for moral resolution. There may be other ways to bring closure to the matter, such as overpowering the other and making him agree to it, but that, by definition is not a moral resolution. The commitment may be only more or less conscious, but it must be discoverable among the disputants. If not, then they have agreed upon nothing and can agree upon nothing.

How can such a seemingly obvious point keep being overlooked? It depends on the starting point. In modern discussions that has typically been, What is the maximum freedom I can exercise? The answer John Stuart Mill gives is that I should be as free as I desire to be until I begin to infringe upon the rights of others.[12]

Modern discussions erroneously assume some midpoint detectable in each conflict to which opposing parties can agree. For example, you want to keep your child from having sexual relations until the child reaches puberty, at least, but the neighborhood pederast wants this child in particular because he or she is still six, that is, exactly the age at which the pederast enjoys most having sex with the child, and that is what makes him happiest. After all, the pederast has rights, too, and certainly the right to happiness. No? Is it because you have a right to protect your child or a right to raise your child as you wish? What is the halfway point between your rights and those of the pederast? When, precisely, does the pederast's exercise of his right begin to interfere with the exercise of yours? And suppose the child likes having sex with him.

Would you really be able to claim, even in America, the fountain of rights, the right to raise your child any way you wished? This is doubtful, not any way you wish. After all, you might think it a good idea for your child to have sex with the pederast. But you are expected to meet certain standards of child care. How are these standards determined? In the same way you can justify keeping the pederast from sexually abusing your child: by raising your child according to what is best for the child.

And what business do we have setting expectations for you with regard to your own child? It is the business that we have together: to provide a wholesome atmosphere for life and living, to assure that the child will mature to be a healthy, contributing member of our society. We need that child and all the others in good health if there is to be a successor generation. We need a place where we can raise our children safely because that is what we want to do. Aristotle would say that is one reason we live together in communities in the first place.

Like it or not, collective intent has a bearing just about anywhere we look, especially in modern life wherein we are all so very interdependent. We seldom look at morality in this way. We are able through a variety of means to overlook and even deny our need for others. We allow our children to wander freely after they reach teenage, and we want a free and open culture until gangs and cults terrify us by luring our children into harmful activities. Then we want the gangs and cults "handled." The concept of rights is useful in the political and legal contexts, but only if we remember that these must be positioned in the wider context of morality. What is moral is determined by how we must interact to meet the challenge of living the best life we know how to live, the best life we can live. We take our world for granted, but it can present rude surprises.

An individual's rights do not check and balance another's rights, nor do an individual's interests. The collected purposes of the members of the society for which members have joined in common pursuit do that. Consider what happens when interests are not only in conflict but also at impasse. How does an arbiter move the disputants? He has to appeal to a shared purpose. Remember the Davises and their fertilized eggs. Remember the pederast. His interest and rights to happiness are readily subordinated to the purpose of proper child rearing.

Section 3. Equality

The members of a real society, one with moral purpose, are equal because they freely embrace the purpose of the society and in doing so become essential to it. Without purpose there is no society, only a collection of humans. How important each member is in the society is not the same as being essential to the society. Membership does not depend on making a contribution to the labors of the society. Obviously, some members contribute more than others to the material well being of the members. If status depended on the degree of contribution, some people would be "more equal" than others. Some members are less able to contribute to the general welfare, but their status is not diminished because of that. We do not consider it just to deprive the poor, weak, or the sick of equal membership.

We cannot anticipate who will be able to contribute, who will not be able to contribute, and who will stop being able to contribute. We live in societies for the assistance membership provides us when we need it, a way of distributing risk, as in an insurance policy. We do not eliminate members of the society when they cannot contribute to the general welfare because most, if not all, members are related in one way or another to those who can contribute, and these contributing members care about the noncontributing ones. Moreover, each of us could and probably will become noncontributing members at some stage of our lives. The support society offers for our care is part of the purpose of civilized societies.

Conditions do arise when the society cannot bear the burden of many noncontributing members. In the United States some claim we are reaching that point with the growing elderly population. There will be decisions about how much of the social resources continue to the elderly, especially if it becomes a matter of depriving the successor generation of essential needs. In most developed nations people are willing to assist others. Every member of the society needs help in one way or another. But most people draw the line when indigents will not even support morally the social goals.

This appears with immigrants, legal and illegal, who come to a country, use its opportunities, never learn the common language, and care only about material gain and not the common life of the society. They may even pay taxes to the government of the society, but if it is only to continue their material gain, they are not voluntarily committed members of the society. They are legally free to do this, but they are not morally equal because they are using the society for their own purposes. And now, of course, it should be clear that not only immigrants can take advantage of this freedom. Others already around with the same lack of social commitment are really not moral members either. Membership has material benefits, but membership is determined not by the material contribution but by the individual's voluntary support of the social purpose.

Taking equality to be free of dominance by others without due regard for its social nature has encouraged thinkers to proclaim, as does Ayn Rand, "the concept of man as a heroic being, with his own happiness as the moral purpose of his life, with productive achievement as his noblest activity, and reason as his only absolute." The man who achieves his moral purpose is the one who achieves his own happiness and, by implication, does not let concern for the happiness of others interfere with his quest for his own. So the hero of *Atlas Shrugged* says, "I swear— by my life and by my love of it—that I will never live for the sake of another man, nor ask another man to live for mine."[13] To sacrifice oneself for the sake of others is to rob oneself of self-esteem, courage, virtue, and honor and turn oneself into a victim, according to *The Fountainhead*.[14] The least act of altruism is morally wrong.

These sentiments inspire certain people, often college freshmen, feeling their independence from family and friends back home. But the allure does not last. For one thing, living the authentic life is exhausting, maybe not for an energetic college student, but for most people most of the time. Even the best of us have to admit from time to time we need to withdraw, to let down our guard, and even ask a favor of another now and then. This is not living for the sake of another man, but it is expecting something from one man for the sake of another, namely oneself. One does not have to live for the sake of another or expect another to live for one's sake in ultimate altruism. One can work with others to accomplish far more than one can alone. In fact, that is what each of us has done and our forebears before us to create the civilization we enjoy.

The heroes of *Atlas Shrugged* and *The Fountainhead* in real life would have to rely on the vast resources of our culture to accomplish what they did in fiction. Imagine the support an architect needs to design any kind of urban building. He relies on a written language developed over centuries, mathematics and physics, the technologies of metallurgy, electronics, masonry, carpentry, ceramics, plumbing, heating and ventilation, and the resources of capital from the banking industry, a tradition of building design from a succession of architects and the universities where research and teaching make skilled people available for the construction. You can try it by yourself and maybe build a mud hut. But through the cumulative refinements of civilization the architect can expect a structure of magnificence, and the same goes for the aeronautical engineer, and the naval architect.

The thread running through the history of equality is freedom from the will of another whether of a king, a class, an elite, a master, a father, mother, sister, or brother. If not properly understood, equality may emerge for some as a "free for all" and "every man for himself." Such an ideal turns out to be false because, paradoxically, the more independent I become, the less I can accomplish. I can really further my own interests only by working with others, and I almost certainly assure my own destruction by not gaining the help and support of others. I cannot expect the help of others unless they believe I am committed to share life with them.

Relying on the civilization one shares with others is inescapable. It is not living for the sake of the others, but it is everyone living for one another for the sake of what each can accomplish for oneself. Doing what is required to maintain this manner of living is being moral. Right and wrong actions are those that support civilized living and those that undermine it. Living peaceably among one's neighbors is right because this promotes a desirable atmosphere among the members of the community. Living disorderly is wrong because it detracts from it. The same goes for living honestly, charitably, thoughtfully and for living dishonestly, uncharitably, and thoughtlessly. This is what it is to live the moral life.

Now the meaning of "equality" should be clear: I am equal in the moral community because I am a member by my choice and so is every other member. No one is there for the sake of another; everyone is there for the sake of what he can do for himself by freely working with the others. Equality is being bound only by one's will and not by the will of another. Its only force is moral force. This is influence we bring upon an individual reminding him of his voluntary commitment to the joint enterprise—traditionally called censure, shame, and social pressure. Society is delicate.

An individual may bind himself to others in many different ways, legally, emotionally, spiritually to name but a few. But these are not ways of being morally bound: they are legal, or psychological, or religious. With this realization, it is easy to understand the present state of morality. People are taking a wait and see attitude on who will emerge as a moral authority to tell them what is right and wrong and compel them to be moral. It doesn't work that way. People have to volunteer to do what is right and not to do what is wrong, willingly supporting human purposes and willingly not undermining them.

Individual choices do not disappear in the moral community, but our purposes are in large measure commonly shared—the need for air, food, water, shelter, love and companionship, procreation and safety. Other purposes vary among us and some of them, including common ones, even change with time as the result of new knowledge and experience. These are often debated. But fundamental purposes remain the same long enough and commonly enough to establish expectations of behavior and stability among the members of the society. At any given time there are a sufficient number of shared purposes so we can make judgments about what people ought to do.

We can do this in a manner that is not idiosyncratic. We can say, for example, Smith ought to eat a healthful diet, and offer as justification that everyone ought to eat a healthful diet. We say this with the understanding that everyone shares the purpose of staying alive as healthy and as long as possible. Our statement that Smith ought to eat a healthful diet applies to Smith as its subject, but it is not because he is Smith; rather, it is because he is a human who shares our need and purpose. So, supposing someone asks, "Why do you say Smith ought to eat a healthful diet?" We can reply, "Because everyone should." And that is the reason Smith should.

Given a certain purpose, it will follow that there are certain things you should do and certain things you should not do to accomplish your purpose. Were Smith to say, "Yes, I want to stay alive and be as healthy as possible as long as I am alive, but why should I eat a healthful diet?", we would surely conclude that Smith did not know what he is talking about or he is being irrational. And so we can see that these judgments are not subjective. Smith has just not taken a wide enough view of his options to see what is at stake.

With moral judgments our purposes, choices, and actions have implications for others as well as for ourselves. They do because the interests of others as well as ours are at stake. We widen the frame, so to speak, to recognize our common purpose. Further, each of us is equal in the sense that no one forces anyone else to participate because each of us seeks the common goal to be obtained by working together. Each of us acts for the good of everyone alike. When considering a course of action, one should ask: Can the conduct I am considering reasonably be expected to be approved by everyone involved? Would everyone who is equally informed of the facts and circumstances and clear about our purposes approve? Would it be good for all of us if anyone and everyone did that? Is the purpose behind the action one we would expect to receive general approval?

For example, because of the risk of a serious water shortage the county has imposed water conservation measures to assure water pressure in case of emergency. People in my neighborhood are expected not to water lawns on Tuesdays, Thursdays and Saturdays. It is past watering time on Friday, the sun has been fierce all day, and I know my lawn will likely not make it without water until Sunday. I also know that no one else in my neighborhood is sprinkling, and so the water pressure will be all right in case there is an emergency. Ought I to water my lawn now? To answer I must ask, would my action receive approval by those affected? Not likely. More likely people will respond, "Look, we all want to save our lawns, but we have the more immediate and pressing need to protect our houses from fire. If we make an exception for you, how will we avoid making exceptions for all of the rest of us?

My watering is wrong because everyone is counting on no one else watering. I have reason to water my lawn: the lawn is dying. But I have a stronger reason not to water: following the watering schedule assures safe water pressure, but only if everyone adheres to the schedule. Only in this way can our purpose be accomplished. And this is true even if I water my lawn at night when no one else can see me do it and no one else is likely to water his own lawn. Indeed, the only way the plan will work is for people to believe everyone is adhering to it, even when one can depart from the plan and get away with it. But once it is abroad that "everyone is doing it" it becomes impossible to maintain a plan requiring people "not to do it." This point cannot be overemphasized in the present moral climate where the only thing wrong is getting caught.

The fundamental elements of ethics are required by the very enterprise of ethics. If we want to talk ethics and be concerned with morality, as it seems we do, then we cannot judge right and wrong, good and bad without agreeing to the principle of individuals, voluntarily committed, to common purpose.

Section 4. Right and Wrong

It is now possible to say what distinguishes right from wrong in a given society. The word "right" has been in use in the English language since the ninth century. Through the centuries it has taken on many meanings, but all hover around the meaning it has always had, and that is "straight." Philosophers and religionists have tried to put the word to many other uses to suit their theories.[15] Keeping to the basic sense, I shall mean by "right" the straightforward notion of "to the point" and by "wrong" the equally straightforward notion of "not to the point." Notice

I am not saying "that which is to the point" as if there is only one thing that is, nor am I saying there is only one thing, the wrong act, that is not. There are many ways to the point and many ways to deviate from it. Now, what is the point? It is where we want to go.

Now, only by way of analogy, consider rules. The rules of a game, when taken together and followed, result in a certain structured event, a game. So a rule has a purpose behind it. Moving in accordance with the purpose of the rule is following it, and following it tends to produce a desired result. The particular way a contestant moves in accordance with the rule to achieve his end may be quite different from the way his opponent does, but both may be moving in accordance with the rules, and this produces the desired result, a complete game of a certain type. If they were to follow a different set of rules, the result could possibly be a game, but it would be a different game. The expected result in the case of society is the furtherance of the best life those voluntarily associated know how to live.

Continuing the rule analogy for a moment enables us to see better the connection between a rule and purpose. There is an old saying, "The exception proves the rule." If anyone thinks about this for more than a moment, his reaction will be puzzlement. How can an exception prove a rule? An exception, it seems, would refute a rule by being a case contrary to the rule. So it would seem, until we learn that "prove" in this case doesn't really mean "to confirm" but rather to "to test" the rule. "Prove" comes from the Latin "probo" which originally meant "to probe" much as a dentist probes our teeth during an examination. The exception tests the rule by making us ask why we have this rule in the first place.

Most societies have some kind of rule against taking the life of another human being such as "Thou shalt not kill" found in the Law of Moses. And most societies make certain exceptions to this rule, notably in the case of killing another human being if necessary to protect one's own life. A few moralists interpret the rule literally to mean that even self-defense is proscribed and one ought not to kill even in self-defense. But this exception tests the rule. What is the purpose of the rule? If it is to protect life, then killing in the protection of life is consistent with it. If it is to end killing, then perhaps the interpretation should be to let others kill us when they take a notion to do so. Presumably one should have no part of killing, and, perhaps, being unwilling to kill, even when it costs one his life, sets some kind of example for would-be killers. But a rule allowing others to kill us would hardly end killing.

Lest it appear morality is merely following rules, remember that morality is not a game but a matter of life and death. Our knowledge of possibilities for us changes, and so do the conditions of our life together. Deciding what is right requires circumspect judgment including a sense of what is expected of each of us to shape the life we seek together. But the rule analogy does suggest that the shape of life we seek determines what is right and what is wrong.

"Right" is not the same as "useful." Confusing the two has contributed substantially to the coarsening of the modern world. It has become common to think whatever serves one's ends is right. When we are trying especially hard to be moral, we qualify this and think whatever in a given situation leads to the greatest happiness for everyone is right. "Do what is best all around." "Do what makes you happy." "Do unto others what you would have them do unto you." Right? Well, you want others to make you happy. In its general, governmental, media form, it is: "Do what promotes the greatest happiness for the greatest number." "Do what gets the most votes." "Do what gets the highest ratings."

Generally, that is how people trying to be moral decide what is right. They try to promote the greatest happiness for the greatest number. But, of course, the pursuit of happiness may be shortsighted and short lived. Those who think that ethics is about the pursuit of happiness may reply that they are not talking about shortsighted happiness but about real happiness. But how do you tell the difference? One reason utilitarian doctrine has had so much appeal is its use of the word "happiness." Those who base their conduct upon pursuit of the best life they can conceive will certainly be happy if they ever achieve it. But this is quite distinct from the modern version of secular contentment known as "happiness."

Some people want to live meaningful lives and find a great deal of unhappiness and pain in the process. Others may live for something they regard a higher purpose than their happiness or even the happiness of the greatest number. For such people their conduct will lead to their ultimate goal in life, and so what is right for them will not be right for the utilitarian in his quest for happiness. The actions required for the protection of life, for example, and actions required for happiness as a life of pleasure are not all compatible. The morality developed over the centuries to advance civilization can hardly be translated into the mere pursuit of happiness. It has required sharing, abstinence, and even sacrifice. Some may call that happiness in the end. In that sense everyone seeks happiness, but that merely makes happiness the achievement of what we want to achieve.

So is everything "relative," as those too lazy to examine the issues are fond of saying? No, there is more to be said. One alternative is to look for the one and only way of life that everyone should pursue, and require conduct that will carry everyone in that direction. This is the position taken by the modern secular thinkers who believe they can discover what that is through scientific thinking about human nature. It is also the position taken by those who believe we humans have natural rights and create laws to secure these so-called natural rights. It is also the position taken by dogmatic religious thinkers who promote and pray for all human beings to recognize the "one true way" these religious thinkers have discovered for us.

There is another alternative. That is to look for the fundamental requirements for any organized society and to require conduct securing a civil life among all people who choose to live and interact with one another, and leave the matter of happiness or ultimate purpose to the individual. We agree to live in basic civility and leave each person alone to find his ultimate purpose or none at all. It appears that we are trying to do something like this in the United States. Is it working? The current moral conflicts here and in other countries trying the same thing make it doubtful. Questions about abortion, homosexuality, suicide, sexuality are not resolvable on a "live and let live" arrangement. Something more is needed for morality to be possible.

It is not possible to omit such key issues by agreeing on a few irrefutable moral rules such as not killing, stealing, lying, and cheating. These alone do not a moral community make. At best they provide a *modus vivendi* for moral subcultures to co-exist or, better, cohabitate. In particular, it provides no basis for the resolution of conflicts arising from differences in religion or world view, and it relies on tolerance to muddle through crises. A person who believes the human embryo is a human being is not going to reach agreement on abortion with a person who believes the human embryo is merely a small mass of cells. In the *modus vivendi* community, both parties believe that killing another human being is wrong. Consequently one party will believe the aborting party is committing murder.

To resolve their conflict in a moral manner, the parties to the conflict must see the issue of abortion in the context of their joint activity as free individuals. Admittedly, it is not readily foreseeable just how conservative

Christians and secular liberals will come to agreement on the issue. But it is readily foreseeable that, unless they sit down together as participants in joint activity regarding procreation and examine their disagreement as participants in joint activity with regard to procreation, there can at best be only acquiescence and political and legal compromise, and we know how unstable that can be.

There is an additional dimension of difficulty here, too. The conservative view on abortion is based on certain beliefs about the nature of humans and the status of human embryos. Since these are not empirically verifiable, the discussion of joint interest in procreation promises to be an extremely difficult one. But the proper understanding of the nature of right and wrong explains what course their discussion will have to take if they wish for a moral resolution. The situation may not be as hopeless as it appears because both the conservative and the liberal positions may be lifted into the framework of their shared societal interest in safe procreation.

Section 5. The Source of Morality

In explaining the source of morality I have had frequent recourse to the phrase "social fabric." As a metaphor it has been convenient, but it will be instructive to make literal sense of it. Fabric, as cloth, is made of interwoven threads, overlapping, crisscrossing, tied, broken and retied. So also is the network of relationships in society—mother and daughter, father and son, sister and brother, aunt and nephew, uncle and niece, husband and wife, lover and lover, caregiver and care receiver, doctor and patient, teacher and student, buyer and seller, neighbor and neighbor, friends of friends, friends of relatives, and all of the crisscrossing relationships such as teacher and cousin, mother and business associate. In each of these a meaningful human relationships exist—supplier of need, provider of help, recipient of care. These are relationships the individuals want maintained usually for specific reasons.

The person who interferes with one of these relationships disrupts a part of what is involved in social living. The relationship of father and son, say, is provided by nature, but without social reinforcement it is really nothing more than biological dependence of the son on the father. Only when that relationship is invested with responsibility in the father for nurture of the son and duties in the son toward the father do we see what in most societies is the full relationship of father and son. These responsibilities and duties are reinforced through the societal need for the relationship of father and son. In this regard society determines the relationship even though the individual father and individual son do make their own specific interpretation of that relationship.

The social roles are performed by each doing what is expected of him, and the acts each performs in that regard are right acts when they conform to the role serving a purpose of the society. No one fills just one role, and no one is locked into a position in society. This is one reason choosing the right action is frequently difficult to do. But one's relationships indicate what one's responsibilities are. It is wrong to interfere with these relationships and the actions they require. Imagine the social destruction in interfering with the relationship between teacher and student, or physician and patient. To the extent each person understands what the social expectations of him and others are, to that extent he is aware of being a member in his society. In all of these roles, performed in accordance with social expectations, its members share social consciousness.

Social consciousness also reveals general or "higher order" relationships among members indicating actions and non-actions expected of individuals just because they are members of the society and share in the common purpose. The general expectation is that one will not interfere with others to the social detriment and, as able, carry one's assigned share of the social burdens.

Frederick Engels describes the lack of social consciousness following the breakdown in social relationships in London in 1844 as follows:

> Hundreds of thousands of men and women drawn from all classes and ranks of society pack the streets of London. Are they not all human beings with the same innate characteristics and potentialities? And do they not all aim at happiness by following similar methods? Yet they rush past each other as if they had nothing in common. They are tacitly agreed on one thing only—that everyone should keep to the right of the pavement so as not to collide with the stream of people moving in the opposite direction. No one even thinks of sparing a glance for his neighbors in the streets. The more that Londoners are packed into a tiny space, the more repulsive and disgraceful becomes the brutal indifference with which they ignore their neighbors and selfishly concentrate upon their private affairs. We know well enough that this isolation of the individual—this narrow-minded egotism—is everywhere the fundamental principle of modern society. But nowhere

is this selfish egotism so blatantly evident as in the frantic bustle of the great city. The disintegration of society into individuals, each guided by his private principles and each pursuing his own aims has been pushed to its furthest limits in London. Here indeed human society has been split into its component atoms.[16]

If this is an appropriate description of London in 1844, it is more appropriate in our current era with greater crowding and further breakdown of traditional relationships among family, friends, and fellow workers. It could be a description of New York City, too, where according to Louis Kronenberger, "It is one of the prime provincialities . . . that its inhabitants lap up trivial gossip about essential nobodies they've never set eyes on, while continuing to boast that they could live somewhere for twenty years without so much as exchanging pleasantries with their neighbors across the hall." If true of New York, then probably it is true of Detroit, St.Louis, and Los Angeles, and perhaps even of middle and small cities, where information and ideas are exchanged electronically by means of telephone, television, fax, and computer networks, leaving people in isolation Engels could not have imagined.

But a common error Engels makes is thinking people, when thrown together by fortuitous circumstances, such as living in a huge metropolis like London, have no meaningful relationships and are isolated. The fact is people relate to one another in a myriad of ways. They did in 1844 and they do today in large cities and in small towns. Indeed, these relationships are inescapable. Some people are related in more ways than others and to more people than others. We see this at weddings and funerals. Almost everyone knows and is known by at least 200 people. The relationships are extremely complex and often not obvious, as when seeming strangers appear at funerals who are later identified as a business partner of the deceased's cousin, or, perhaps the daughter of the former nurse of the deceased who came to help her mother on busy days.

Often we respond to others spontaneously with feelings of gratitude or guilt. We are pleased by what someone has done for us or we regret we did not please one who has pleased us. Weddings are the best place to see this. Everyone invited is there for some reason. It is usually someone or a friend or relative of such a one who has loved and supported the bride or the groom. What Engels did not see is that people form relationships no matter what their economic or governmental structure may be. The people on the streets of London had friends and family elsewhere if not with them on the street, and there is no reason to think people are related just by virtue of being on the streets of London at the same time. We are familiar with this in the way we now speak of "the black community" or "the business community" as ways of referring to people who have a common interest whether they live next door to each other or not, whether they walk the same city streets together or not.

What bothered Engels was his belief that we need a new economic order imposed to make us behave decently toward everyone around us. What he and Marx failed to see, in their genuine humanistic interest, was that without bonding of mutual assent born of common purpose there is no basis for moral behavior toward one another. But it is not just Marx and Engels who fail to see this. Those in modern America consumed by interest in "individual rights" make this error, too. They reason that if we can just make everyone acknowledge everyone else's rights, then everything in our society will go well. But without a purpose in acknowledging the rights of another, we will not do so, and, in fact, we do not, except when forced to do so by government and law.

What is missing is the purpose that results from the pyramiding of relationships developed in the course of living. What is missing is the assent of individuals to a purpose they acknowledge as worthwhile, one they intend to further by each doing his part. The present situation is one wherein people live and work in a governmental and economic order they are willing to use provided it suits their individual purposes, much as employees of a company who do what they have to do for a paycheck but do not make it their business to further the company. They do not see they have any stake in it beyond getting their pay. There is no assent to a common purpose by partners working for mutual benefit.

Perhaps the keen sense of competition in the commercial world has contributed to this state of affairs. Each of us lives and works to provide what each wants, but balks when it comes time to support the "system" by being honest when we have no fear of being caught. The attempts of government to supply a common purpose ring hollow because they are superimposed on social purpose rather than implementations of it. As a result we live for what we sense is our own purpose and use "the system" for that purpose. There is no need to be loyal to something we use; we value such a thing only so long as it is useful for getting what we do value.

Whether these feelings are natural or learned for the sake of improved social action we need not answer. All we need do is note such responses exist and from such responses relationships develop and lead people to cooperate for mutual purposes. In turn, we learn from such cooperative relationships that everyone in the society can act in a concerted manner by respecting one another's interests, even when we can get away without doing so. Moral relationships begin with mutual interest, cooperation, support, and common needs and goals. Think of how a coach can make demands, vigorously criticize, and drive the athlete, and think of how the athlete feels about the coach. They can give and take a great deal from each other and build a rich relationship because they are both working for the same thing, the athlete's success.

Perhaps I may be forgiven a very personal anecdote if it helps explain the interpersonal connectedness I am claiming is the foundation of morality. I remember seeing some 10 year old neighbor boys enthusiastically teach my three and a half year old son a skill game. They cheered him on and became as excited as he was when he could throw the ball in the right direction. I became very close to those boys and loved them for what they were doing. Because of this learning they shared with my son and the relationship I have with my son all of us became one for a moment and closer to one another for good. Think of how we treat one another when our relationship is like that. We are in an easy give and take. We do for one another, share knowledge and skill, lend a helping hand.

You and your neighbor can do certain things only together—move a tree too heavy for one of you, pull in a big fish, stalk a wolf, harvest a bumper crop before it spoils. Your neighbor knows how to dress a wound and to relieve the infection. You have an infected wound. Do you expect your neighbor to help heal you or share his knowledge to heal you? Why? Do you expect a doctor or a pharmaceutical company to help heal you? Well, for a fee. They have to live, too. But we would not expect any of them to keep their healing techniques a secret to your detriment. Why not? Because that would not be civilized.

Is this all based on some quid pro quo? Do we, can we measure the exact worth of one favor, so we can give back just the exact amount of return favor? It doesn't seem so. And that is how human relationships become enriched and have surprising consequences. One may find he is more obligated than he thought or has obligated one to himself more or less than he thought. To manage this we create relationships within which certain expectations lie—friends, close friends, lovers, fellow citizens. These relationships intersect, overlap and conflict. They have their own duties and privileges, some stronger, some weaker, some overriding. So we have to "weigh" to decide what is right. But all is based in one way or another upon preserving and possibly deepening our social rapport with one another. Stealing from another destroys or substantially deteriorates it. So does lying to one another, breaking promises, and abusing social institutions.

Acting in immoral ways detracts from the benefits we gain being in moral rapport. Acting in moral ways builds that rapport.

Notes

1. Aristotle, *The Nicomachean Ethics*, Book X, Baltimore, Maryland, Penguin Books, 1963.
2. Chester E. Finn, Jr., "Ten Tentative Truths," Keynote Address at the Center of the American Experiment Inaugural Converence, St. Paul, Minnesota, April 4, 1990.
3. Edward T. Hall, *Beyond Culture*, New York, Doubleday Anchor Books, 1989, 46ff.
4. *Ibid*, p. 46.
5. *Ibid*, pp. 51-2.
6. Thomas Hobbes, *Leviathan*, New York, Oxford University Press, 1947, Chs. XIII and XIV.
7. Kurt Baier, *The Moral Point of View*, New York, Random House, Inc., pp. 119-20.
8. Alan M. Dershowitz, *Contrary to Popular Opinion*, New York, Pharos Books, 1992, pp. 221-3.
9. Alfred Louis Kroeber, *The Nature of Culture*, Chicago: University of Chicago Press, 1952.
10. Mary Midgley, *Heart and Mind,* New York, St. Martin's Press, 1981.
11. Not all groups of people have attained this level. These groups I prefer to term "pre-moral" communities wherein group conduct is organized and directed by means other than mutual assent to purpose.
12. John Stuart Mill, "On Liberty," Introductory, in *John Stuart Mill,* Gertrude Himmelfarb (ed.), New York, Viking Press, 1983.
13. Ayn Rand, *Atlas Shrugged,* Garden City, New York, International Collectors Library, 1957, Vol. II, p. 1061.
14. Ayn Rand, *The Fountainhead*, New York, New American Library (Signet Edition), 1968, pp. 680 ff.
15. R. G. Collingwood, *The New Leviathan,* New York, Oxford University Press, 1958, pp. 111ff.
16. Quoted in the introduction by Eric and Mary Josephson (eds.), *Man Alone: Alienation in Modern Society,* New York, Dell Publishing Co., Inc., 1966, p. 32.

Chapter IV

ℰℭ

Religion as a Source of Morality: Celestial Navigation

"We have just enough religion to make us hate
But not enough to make us love one another"—Jonathan Swift

Religion and civilization have developed together. The philosopher Alfred North Whitehead once remarked that even modern science could not have appeared without the idea of God as a sustainer of a unified and orderly world. Our earliest views of nature and our place in it have been religious in nature. So have our views of how we ought to conduct ourselves. The morality of most peoples is intimately related to their religious beliefs which in turn are major determinants of their cultures. Religious beliefs are deeply imbedded in the cultures they help create and maintain, and they also affect their cultures in many ways. One cannot easily say where the sacred ends and the secular begins, or where religion ends and morality begins. Also, how people live and the role of their religion in determining how they live vary from culture to culture.

No one religion can serve as a model for the study of religion or for the study of religious ethics. Some religions are monotheistic, most religions are polytheistic, and some religions have no god at all. The apologists for monotheistic and polytheistic religions in the main describe moral conduct as that which is according to divine command. Acting in a certain way is right because God commands it or because it is pleasing to the gods. Acting in another way is wrong because is violates God's commandment or because it is displeasing to the gods. The apologists for atheistic religions in the main describe moral conduct as that according to "enlightenment." All religions compare in this sense of enlightenment: there is one true way. It may be the way commanded by God, or the way that pleases the gods, or the way of the enlightened. But there is one true way.

The unique characteristic of religious ethics is the fundamental belief that what is right and what is wrong is determined by a source and sanction outside the individual. It matters not how we "feel" about an action or what our inclinations are. There is a real difference between right and wrong, and the difference is determined by something other than ourselves. For religions holding to a doctrine of God the Creator, we do not even exist in our own right but only as God's creatures. It is presumed to follow that we ought to do what God desires. We do not own ourselves or the world we inhabit; rather, we hold them in trust for the Creator and ought, therefore, to govern our actions by respect for the One upon whom we depend for our existence.

Again, an act I perform is right, not because any person or group thinks it is, but because it is fitting according the world as it is interpreted by religious doctrine. There is a real distinction between right and wrong independent of what we think. When we think something is right, but it is not according to doctrine, we are mistaken. We may not know it at the time we are acting and may never know it, but it is nevertheless wrong. There is such a thing as human nature, and we must strive to fulfill our destinies by living a life of virtue. We are to live with justice, courage, temperance, and consideration for others. The unfair one, the thief, the coward, the libertine and the oppressor all fail themselves. The universe is so ordered.

Religions differ in how their sacred scriptures describe the world. I shall present some ways in which the major religions compare, and, though they may not be precise, they are useful in understanding ethics.

First, most, if not all, major religions require commitment and self-dedication to the doctrines and, above all, to the deity if there is supposed to be one. In the Holy Bible we read: "Yahweh is a jealous God," and

"Love the Lord your God with all your heart, with all your mind; and your neighbor as yourself." In the Bhagavad-Gita, Chapter XVII, Lord Krishna declares:

> And whatsoever deeds he doeth—fixed
> In Me, as in his refuge—he hath won
> For Ever and For ever by My grace
> Th' Eternal Rest! So win thou! In thy thoughts
> Do all thou dost for Me! Renounce for Me!
> Sacrifice heart and mind and will to Me! In faith of Me
> All dangers thou shalt vanquish, by My grace,
> But, trusting to thyself and heeding not,
> Thou can'st but perish!

In the Glorious Koran we read: "he who cleaveth firmly unto God is already directed in the right way" And in the Buddhist prayer, the Mahavagga Sutta:

> How blest the happy solitude
> Of him who hears and knows the truth!
> How blest is harmlessness towards all,
> And self-restraint towards living things!
> How blest from passion to be free,
> All sensuous joys to leave behind!
> Yet far the highest bliss of all
> To quit the Illusion false—'I am.'

Self-surrender leads to a new life, either as a gift from God or as the result of truth discerned and discipline followed. This idea is, perhaps, captured in the familiar phrase "born again."

There is a second comparable. Self-commitment to God or the true path requires certain conduct. The great religions of the world differ widely in how they state it, but they all teach that we attain the highest form of life through a fuller relationship to our fellow human beings. In Buddhist scripture we find: "Let you heart so shine that having left the world to enter into so well-taught a doctrine and discipline, you may be respectful, affectionate, and hospitable to all." Mohammed commands: "Give unto the poor and the orphan and the bondsman for His sake, saying we feed you for God's sake only; from you we desire no recompense, nor any thanks." Jesus commands "Love thy neighbor as thyself" and teaches that "Inasmuch as ye have done it unto these the least of my brethren, ye have done so unto me." And Confucius says, "In seeking a foothold for self, love finds a foothold for others; seeking light for itself, it enlightens others also."

The Ten Commandments found in Exodus 20 are especially instructive. As the deliverer of an entire people, God commands in these words:

> I am the Lord Your God, who
> brought you out of Egypt, out of
> the land of slavery.
> You shall have no other gods before me.
> You shall not make for yourself an idol in the form of anything in heaven above or on the earth beneath or in the waters below. You shall not bow down to them or worship them; for I, the Lord your God, am a jealous God, punishing the children for the sin of the fathers to the third and fourth generation of those who hate me, but showing love to a thousand generations of those who love me and keep my commandments.
> You shall not misuse the name of the Lord your God, for the Lord will not hold anyone guiltless who misuses his name.
> Remember the Sabbath day by keeping it holy. [The remainder of verse eight is omitted here.]
> Honor your father and your mother, so that you may live long in the land the Lord your God is giving you.
> You shall not murder.
> You shall not commit adultery.
> You shall not steal.
> You shall not give false testimony against your neighbor.
> You shall not covet your neighbor's house. You shall not covet your neighbor's wife, or his manservant or maidservant, his ox or donkey, or anything that belongs to your neighbor.[1]

The relationship between the person and God is defined and demanded in the first four commandments. God is addressing all of the people He delivered and commanding each to attune himself in the same way to God. In turn, the relationship of each person to the others is defined and demanded in the remaining six Commandments: honor your father and mother; you shall not murder, commit adultery, steal, give false testimony against your neighbor, or covet your neighbor's wife and property. These commandments are elaborated in the following chapters of Exodus, and they provide much, if not all, needed to establish and operate an ordered society, along with directions for proper worship of God. The social order is ordained by God and operated by the faithful in the manner He has specified.

Why these commandments? For the Hebrews this was hardly a permissible question. Exodus, 20: 18-21 records:

> When the people saw the thunder and lightening and heard the trumpet and saw the mountain in smoke, they trembled with fear. They stayed at a distance and said to Moses, "Speak to us yourself and we will listen. But do not have God speak to us or we will die."
>
> Moses said to the people, "Do not be afraid. God has come to test you, so that the fear of God will be with you to keep you from sinning."
>
> The people remained at a distance, while Moses approached the thick darkness where God was.

God intended the people to be afraid, and they were afraid and not about to ask any questions.

There are religious moralists teaching today that would be content with that: it is enough that God has commanded it. This may be why religious ethics commands much less attention in modern times when it is fashionable to question any and all authority, even God. But it is obvious that there is much more in this chapter of Exodus. First of all, why are the commandments defining the Hebrews' relationship to God given in the same time and place as the commandments for living? Second, while it may be obvious that God may command His people to worship Him in any way He chooses, why does He command the Hebrews to live in just the manner He defines? Is there anything special about adultery or stealing that God should enjoin them? Adulterers abound and seem to flourish in the world today, and, judging from the media, they are admired.

It appears that the fear God intended to instill in the people was to help them keep the law, not to make the people just do something, anything, out of fear. The Commandments are right, not because God commands them; God commands them because they are right. Anyone who accepts the relationship to God as defined in the first four Commandments should obey all of the Commandments because his God has commanded them, but that is not what makes the Commandments right.

What makes them right stems from the context of deliverance. God tells the people He delivered them from danger and now tells them how to live to be delivered from the perils they will face the rest of this life. This makes Judaism similar to all of the other great religions of the world: one finds salvation by living in a certain manner. The manner prescribed varies from religion to religion, but the basic idea is the same: get into the proper relationship with ultimate reality, live a moral life, and you will be fulfilled.

The moral life outlined in the Ten Commandments is unique to the historical experience of the Hebrews. The deliverance out of Egypt is only a small part of the context establishing the meaning of the gift of the Mosaic law. But from the study of ethics it is clear that the content of the Mosaic law is fundamental to any society of human beings. While it may be possible to imagine a society of adulterers, it is not possible to imagine a society of adulterers going on for a very long time. It is true that most modern societies are showing a high tolerance for adultery, but the tolerance is possible only because a substantial portion of their members still respect traditional marriage as it is instituted in those societies. When adultery becomes extensive and prolonged in any society, major societal problems arise. Marriage, whether monogamous or polygamous, deteriorates, responsibility for child rearing diminishes, the lot of the divorced or abandoned spouse, especially the woman, declines, and conflicted social relations among spouses and lovers arise.

Comparable remarks may be made about stealing and murder. Most civilized societies can tolerate a certain amount, but when they become extensive, we begin to speak of "moral decay" and feel unsafe on our streets and in our homes. We want something done about it. We cannot trust our institutions, our government, our banks, our professionals for the lying and dishonesty. We become cynical: "Everybody is on the take." The Ten Commandments are about the backbone of any society.

The commandment to honor father and mother presents a matter of special interest for the theme of this book—that morality is the way each of us conducts the joint venture with others to maximize our life. To understand this commandment, we have to remember its context is a relatively simple and rather early society. This is not to say that it does not apply to modern societies, but that our understanding of it begins more easily by remembering its original context and stripping away the layers of modernity that make us forget the fundamentals of society.

Honoring father and mother includes obeying them, something all serious parents try to teach their children to do. Why? One reason is the child's own good. If the child runs into a busy street and does not listen to a calling parent the child may be injured or killed. If the child does not listen to other warnings of the parents and does not bother to learn what the parent has to teach, the child further endangers his life and risks missing important possibilities. The child who will not learn from his parents how to plant crops or to hunt and fish or otherwise provide food will starve to death.

Because of the way we are made as humans, parents are the ones most likely to care whether their child learns these things and many others essential to the child's survival and spiritual well being. Just why this is so is only now beginning to be understood by scientists. We have finally put aside the notion of survival of the fittest long enough to realize humans respond to one another in complex ways, that our genetic structure in addition to hunger, fear, and rage may include altruistic emotions, especially for our children. Also, something we call "bonding" is known to exist. The bonding created between a nursing mother and her child may be chemical in nature. Psychological bonding occurs in many forms. The closer people are the closer the bonding.

But it is not necessary to refer to bonding between parent and child to establish the moral importance of the parental relationship. If parents did not for the most part take the parental role seriously, whatever the reason, very few helpless infants would live long enough to attain self-sufficiency. Whatever it is that makes parents endure childbearing and child care we know must be very strong in most humans. When we think of what some people will endure to become parents, we know the feeling of parent for child usually is very strong. It is less clear about the feeling of child for parent. Hence, the wisdom of the Commandment. The child who does not hearken to the advice of the parent, the single most qualified and committed teacher the child is ever likely to have, will have little chance of flourishing or even surviving.

We can see in the wisdom expressed in the commandment for the welfare of the child something more. In the press of meeting our momentary desires, and even when we try to think ahead, we usually do not look far enough. We know that, even when we try very hard, we are not able to take in everything we should to make solid plans and decisions. We say we are "shortsighted." What is more, we often cannot, do not know how, to take in everything. Think of the last time you saw an auto accident, how hard it was to grasp the situation. It all happens so fast. Life is extremely complex. We tend to live in tight circles because of that. Even as adults we cannot help but act as children in not seeing what the more experienced in their wisdom can see. Some theologians have called this our original sin. We can see how dependent we are on others to live in expected ways, to share with us what they know from their experience, their hard learned lessons in life. How but with the support of others can we expect to make it? How but by honoring one another can we expect the support to continue?

Short of opening a full scale apology for the Ten Commandments, we can leave as an exercise for those interested to decide which, if any, of Commandments can be omitted from a civilized society. Could a society long endure condoning or even tolerating murder as a solution to disputes or as a means of obtaining individual goals? Could a society of liars, bearers of false witness, be inhabitable? Could a person live much of a life in a society where his spouse or any of his possessions, however meager, were free for the taking by anyone who wanted them? And what kind of atmosphere would we have, even where people didn't take things, if still we knew they coveted them? Better for domestic tranquility to train ourselves to regulate our desires as well as our actions.

It seems inherent in the idea of a creator god commanding his people to behave in a certain way that they would not so behave unless commanded. The Ten Commandments, as they are structured, reveal our tendency as humans to live in the short range. We tend not to honor our parents and one another and need to be told by an external source to do so. We do not look far enough ahead and maybe we couldn't see anyway. How many of us wish we had listened to our parents and our elders and honored them more?

Also, implied is the need to get beyond the present in another way. We have to recognize our need for one another in a way that it is not natural for us. We may be able to cooperate with those immediately around us who love us and whom we love. We may be able to give them special regard and honor them. But it is difficult to go beyond others who help and support us. We don't need them, we say, if we bother at all to think of them and our relationship to them. But just as no one member of a family can long endure without the support of the family, so no one family can long endure without other families in the society who, in supporting themselves, also support other families by the society they help create through their constructive living. This dual notion of external sanction and respect for others is amplified in each religion.

The great religions also compare in that the ultimate reality they present transcends any and all of us as something we would not ordinarily regard worthwhile, but something, once understood, we would not give up even if it required sacrifice from us, something beyond human utility.

Thus, a moral duty to one's fellow human requiring self-sacrifice may be justified by the ultimate reality, even if not by immediate utility. In Nathaniel Hawthorne's *The Scarlet Letter,* Hester Prynne bore the burden of the scarlet "A" for adulteress, even when she could have helped herself by publicly confessing who fathered her child born outside wedlock.[2] She suffered the severest scorn the outraged public could express. She, no doubt, did not want to sully the excellent public reputation of the father, the Reverend Dimmesdale. But the main reason was that she believed she had done him wrong by allowing the adultrous relationship. The wrong was in the pain she had caused him in the eyes of God. This was pain caused by a reality far beyond the puritanical community they inhabited because there the reverend was profoundly admired. But he suffered, despite his reputation, because of his sense of divine justice. And Hester, too, though clearly not as confident of divine retribution as Dimmesdale, chose to protect him because of the wrong she caused him in violation of the divine order.

Similarly, in the film noir, "Mildred Pierce," Mildred who could not do enough for her daughter, Veda, paid dearly.[3] Veda became a greedy monster contemptuous of Mildred. Some feminists have criticized the film's implied "values," having Mildred to pay the price for being uppity, seeking a business career, and neglecting her husband, Bert, in order to gain wealth, respectability, and love from her ungrateful daughter. Considering the film was made in 1944, there is probably considerable merit in that criticism. But Bert cared about Mildred despite her divorcing him for utilitarian and materialistic reasons and using other men in the process. Bert picks up the pieces, even after Veda murders Mildred's second husband who was having an affair with her, Mildred's own daughter. Even then Mildred tries to take the rap for Veda. Failing that, Mildred is devastated, but Bert is there for her. Why should he be and why does that make things "right" at the end of the film?

The answer stands in stark contrast to the materialism and selfishness at the center of the film: Bert remains true to his wife because in the grand scheme of things it is right for him to sacrifice his immediate happiness (after all, he had his chance for that with another woman in the film) out of duty to his wife despite her tragic character. To be sure, Bert has to be there in the end for the required "happy ending" of all films of that era, even the films noirs. But it only works, admittedly, faintly because of our sense of an order beyond "I scratch your back and you scratch mine." The individual in his quest for salvation is involved in the lives of fellow human beings. This may mean limitation of desire, but this is sanctioned by the ultimate reality not readily seen. This reality may not be readily seen, but nevertheless is revealed to us, and we can recognize it.

This brings us to another comparable among religions. Each has a body of sacred writings providing a continuing source of inspiration on moral questions and containing wisdom revealed through the ages by holy persons, the collective experience of the people's ancestors, and, according to certain religions, by God himself. It is really impossible to encapsulate the morality of any of the great religions. Life is complex, moral problems multiply, times change to pose new moral dilemmas to ponder. Scriptures stand as the infallible source for answers. The faithful may have to look again and again, but they agree here they will find the answers to their moral questions. Some of the faithful will insist all questions are literally answered and some will insist that interpretation is required. The problems of exegesis are familiar but beyond our scope. Suffice it to say, adherence to sacred scriptures makes a substantial difference between religious ethics and secular ethics.

From a philosophical perspective the ethical positions of the religious have both strengths and weaknesses. Looking as we are for a foundation for morality, we cannot but be attracted to the featured strengths of religious ethics. Each of the great religions has its natural order and in it there is a true path, a safe and proper course to steer toward salvation from the perils of this life. For some religions it means getting us safely to the next life and for others it means making this life meaningful. Anyway, there is ultimate, unquestionable authority. We may have to explore to find it, but we know it is in the holy scriptures. There is the direction to love, respect, aid, somehow cherish one's neighbor, that is, someone outside your own family, and so one major cornerstone of social harmony is an integral part of the ethical portion of the great religions.

One last major strength of religious ethics is the external reference to a deity or a higher attainable state, as in Buddhism, keeping us focused on goals greater than those of our base nature, our limiting self-centeredness. The significance of this for ethics can hardly be overestimated. While our human purposes may be a guide to right and wrong, that is, actions we take supporting our purposes are right and those undermining them are wrong, we ourselves may not always choose goals best for us. Taking the "God's eye" point of view of holy scriptures, may help us beyond our shortsightedness as humans. We are led by our religions to seek the greatest potentialities for us. And since we are thus led beyond ourselves, there is an implied objective basis for the difference between right and wrong. We have become accustomed in modern times to act on the basis of "how it feels." We rarely stop to ask whether that is how we should feel, but when we do, we have to consider what should be our guide. Religions answer with their glimpses of ultimate reality.

It is difficult for the modern person to subscribe to the ethics of a religion. Despite similarities in ethics, the great religions tend to remain unto themselves, some even claiming to be the sole way to salvation through their particular beliefs and practices. While some of the ethical teachings of the religions may be appealing, without the sanction of the whole mythic structure of any one religion there seems to be little offered that is unavailable through rational means. This raises questions about whether any one religion or even all of them could provide a foundation for the ethics of modern societies whose members are not all of the same religion or of any religion at all.

Furthermore, no one religion has to date shown enough broad appeal as a candidate to provide the moral foundation for a modern society. Even within religions there are divisions, and sects. Most apologists for their religions would say it is not the task of a religion to appeal to individual believers, and that it is for the individual to come to terms with the faith. But our question is a practical one. When and how will this take place in sufficient numbers so that we can be a moral community established on a foundation provided by one religion? In modern times societies are becoming more rather than less complex in the number of religions and sects they contain.

Some of the dominant forces in contemporary societies are resulting in greater secularization than in the past. Governments have become far greater influences in our lives than ever, reaching into every facet from childbirth to elder care. Their strength lies in their mass appeal, and, with few exceptions, that means ignoring, not just religious differences, but religion altogether. The other dominant force having the same effect is the mass media. It is true that government and the mass media make allowances as they are able for the diversity of religions, but the central thrust of their programming appeals to the greatest number at any given time. That can be done only by staying on the surface of the commonplace.

What would one really expect, anyway? The central objective of both government and the media is mass appeal, for the former to stay in power and the latter to make money. The goal of entertainment is hardly commensurate with the quest for ultimate reality. The same is true for mass marketing and most commercial enterprise. It may be that secularization has gone too far to expect religions to be a moral factor in our societal life, and if so, it is even less likely for any one religion to be a moral factor.

Probably the most telling objection concerning religion as the source of morality is that frequently we have to ask ourselves what scripture is telling us about our ethical questions. We are not willing to accept any moral claim just because it is suppose to be based in religion. For example, some Christians proscribe sexual relations between same sex partners by relying on scriptural passages such as Genesis 19:1-25 and Leviticus 18:22 which categorically condemn such relations. But other Christians are far less certain. They believe they can find a scriptural basis for tolerance and possibly even condonation of homosexual practice in the respect for others found in the teaching to love (agape) one's neighbor. If not there, then at least they wish to argue that Christianity is silent on the matter because the moral code cited in Genesis and Leviticus was for another time, a time when population increase was a priority.

Christian marriage has undergone a transformation among most Protestant denominations. In Matthew 5:34 Jesus says, "But I tell you that anyone who divorces his wife, except for marital unfaithfulness, causes her to become an adulteress, and anyone who marries the divorced woman commits adultery." This is a very strict teaching. Christians adhered to it the best they could for a very long time. Roman Catholics have adhered to an even stricter doctrine: that there can be no divorce whatsoever, and the only way a man and woman who have held themselves out as married can be separated is by proof that the marriage was only apparent and not proper in the eyes of the Roman Catholic Church. While most Christian denominations and most civil authorities have for years acknowledged much wider grounds for divorce, the State of New York restricted the grounds for divorce to adultery only. Even New York has relented.

These people, many of whom call themselves Christians, have decided on moral grounds that the earlier teaching, even in holy scripture, was morally intolerable, that there are other valid reasons for divorce ranging from incompatibility to no fault at all required from either party. No doubt new thinking in psychology has changed attitudes, and the idea that there is only one man for one woman seems singularly naive. It is clear we will not accept just any kind of religious dictate. If we are going to live by our religion, its specific teachings must make sense somewhere or have the promise of making sense to us ethically. So there appears to be something else at work besides literal readings from scripture. To the extent something else is operative, we must acknowledge the application of reason to the exposition of religious ethics.

That people in love with science find it difficult to believe, that powerful forces are at work in our society making it difficult even if we wanted to believe, these facts themselves do not go to the validity of any or all religions. People often do not believe what they should. The real question is whether in our quest for an ethical foundation for modern societies there is a role for religions and their ethical teachings. By this I do not mean to ask whether there is a role for watered down religion, but whether there is a role that religion as such, as living viable faith, can serve in building an ethical foundation for modern civilization. It would be cavalier to throw religion to the winds. Religion has been the source of ethical living for countless millions of people. Can religion help in dealing with the contemporary moral crisis?

It will facilitate an answer to these questions by concentrating for the time being just on the idea of religion as following the will of God. "What does your God desire for human beings?" Is it something different from what a moral person desires for himself? Most theists would say it is. It results from taking a certain body of scripture seriously and living according to its tradition and teachings. Taking scripture as the revealed word of God makes the difference between how a religious person will act and how a nonreligious person will act. The religious person believes something the nonreligious person does not. He believes he is commanded by God to act in a certain way knowable only in scriptures revealed by God.

I have defined morality as the way a group of people furthers its social purpose. Collective action is required to further the social purpose. The social purpose may be either well chosen or not. The object of living, of course, is to have the purpose best for each and all members of the society. To the extent religious people have something to offer in the selection of social purpose they should be invited to participate as we refine our social purpose. God is commonly understood as a being of perfect goodness and perfect wisdom. What God has revealed, therefore, He must have intended for our edification. In this way a religion may contribute to the moral life of a society.

For some religious people God enforces moral behavior by promising to reward and punish as one does right and wrong according to His will. For others, God is not an enforcer so much as obligor by virtue of His having created them. Either way God encourages moral behavior, especially that not seen or easily enforceable such as not stealing or fornicating when one can get away with it without other people knowing. Motivating people to do what is right is entirely consistent with the expectations of a moral society. More importantly, for some religious people the hope of divine sanction brings forth certain moral conduct such as self-sacrifice which would not be expected in the natural course of social activity.

Perhaps the religious person is saying he has certain duties to observe that others do not. If these are merely additional duties and do not conflict with the duties implied by social expectation, that is, do not interfere with living, such as ritual observances, then they are of no consequence morally. The religious duty some believe they have to refrain from the use of birth control devices is somewhat different. This could easily become a matter of considerable social consequence should there really be a problem of overpopulation. When religious duties conflict with what the nonreligious person considers one's duties, some resolution is required. The religious person may not force his special duties on other members of the society in which he lives because he is then acting without regard for shared social purpose. Societal cooperation for mutual benefit is the essence of morality.

We are having conflicts between secular society and certain religious communities on matters like abortion and homosexuality mainly because some religious persons see their duties as absolute and properly defining of society. Which community comes first, the religious one or the secular one? That is a matter of history now. At one time it was possible for religious communities to define the social purpose based in their interpretation of scriptures. It now appears, that the shoe is on the other foot. There is no logical primacy, only the fact of secularization. Consequently, the present role for the religions of the world is to try to convince the members of society to accept their views on what our social purposes should be.

All people should be welcome in an ethical society to add to our refinements of social purpose. This will always be a matter of ongoing investigation. All points of view should be welcome lest we deprive ourselves of opportunity for better living and vision for what is possible for us. The God's eye point of view of religions, what Spinoza called *sub specie aeternitas*, is uniquely valuable to humans because they tend to become wrapped in the immediate present. Some religious directions turn out to be where we should have been going all along. As an example, we are beginning to see that, had we retained the respect invoked for God's creation, we would not have the environmental problems we now have. As mere mortals we could not see what we were doing to the world until now when we are wondering whether it is too late to do anything about it. Even now we are relying on our own technological devices to save us rather than trying to preserve the creation as we found it.

The idea of revelation creates a duality of knowledge—that which we can know ourselves and that which can only be made known to us by God through inspired writing. The latter takes us beyond our human limitations and tells us we may aspire to something greater than we can see, that life is not merely what our senses tell us. Our social purpose as humans should be informed by revelation, so the possibilities for our lives will not be limited and workaday but noble and commensurate with divine purpose. How the latter bears on human morality may be illustrated with an example.

I had the privilege of knowing Dean Rusk who served as Secretary of State during the Kennedy administration. He told me about a personal experience during the Cuban missile crisis. The United States and the Soviet Union were in a face off, and they had come to the moment of truth in their negotiations. Since neither side would back down, atomic war would likely ensue with mutually assured destruction and probably the whole world with it. In the War Room President Kennedy asked each person present to go out of the room for twenty minutes to decide for himself whether to recommend an atomic strike on the Soviet Union. Secretary Rusk said he found himself in the hall going over his Presbyterian Catechism recalling the response to the question, What is the purpose of man?

There are purposes we set for ourselves such as getting the Soviet missiles out of Cuba, but is it for some set of humans to decide the fate of all mankind? To decide what to recommend Dean Rusk wanted to know what we are supposed to make of our lives and was starting an atomic war consistent with that. Most of us can avoid asking such questions. We can set our goals and live as we like, but are we making the most of our lives? Religions try to answer this question by revealing a purpose beyond what we would ordinarily seek on our own, even surpassing our understanding, a vision calling forth from us a striving for perfection according to the ideal of the particular religion. A religious ideal claims an absolute status, implying that living in pursuit only of it defines the right way to live.

We can consider in contrast the typical ideal of the moral life, social harmony. Taking harmony as the end of morality can be dangerous. Bees in a beehive get along well, but their existence is limited in contrast to human life. On the other hand, humans could be made to get along well through regular doses of Prozac or heavy sodium as described in Walker Percy's *The Thanatos Syndrome* or, for that matter, by having the members of a group trained to settle for the material comforts of modern life and not ask for more. Yet this kind of living makes us ask, Is that all? And if we don't ask, we acquiesce in the modernist syndrome settling for what's new, what's hot, what's diverting, what's "interesting."

We crave something more. Religions claim to supply it, but their ideals are imprecise, requiring interpretation, and, for some religions requiring belief in unperceived realities. The confirmation of these realities may be found in the quality of life that follows from believing in them. From here the matter becomes extremely speculative, and so, being engaged in rational inquiry, we are forced leave it. But this review of religious ethics has taught us that social purpose, our business together as human beings, ranges broadly, from meeting the simplest needs of the individual to meeting the highest needs for life's meaning.

With or without the aid of religion, we must consider the "moral potential" of humans. Together humans can set and attain higher goals than any one of them could alone. Conceiving goals beyond those meeting our immediate needs requires the greatest possible awareness of possibilities; otherwise, the goals selected are born of ignorance and complacency. Religion can take us beyond ourselves, beyond matters most people think about in their daily lives. Since religion can do this, there should always be a place at the table in a moral society for any and all religions.

The purpose of mankind, the role and place of mankind in the universe is a central theme of most major religions. This is usually stated in the form of God's purpose for mankind—created in God's image, children of God—or shown through example in lives of holy persons called saints. Even without specific reference to a transcendent God or reality, human purpose and possibilities are shown through ideal or idealized lives—the Buddha, gurus, prophets, and saints.

Belief in ideals can bring about moral realities. For example, the slaves in America had faith that God would liberate them just as He had liberated the ancient Hebrews from Egypt. It is easy to imagine certain slaves saying they can't "see" that possibility, given the harsh realities around them. But in a real sense they would have been quite mistaken and would likely have made wrong choices because of their lack of vision. History, art, and literature also serve to broaden our vision. We see men and women at their best and worst in moments of high drama. We can make moral decisions taking these moments to heart. We can see the dangers of family rivalry in the lives of young people as in Shakespeare's "Romeo and Juliet," or the folly of vanity in "King Lear," or the consequences of greed in Ibsen's "An Enemy of the People."

Models such as the fallen condition of mankind illustrated in the story of Adam and Eve in Eden and the perfectibility of man as in the myth of progress and Marxism also suggest possibilities and stimulate reflection. Their inherently speculative nature have made many talk of human purposes rather than Purpose. But the person who looks for pervasive themes such as these and for the great dimensions in human affairs, persons such as Sophocles, Dante, Omar Khayam, Mahatma Ghandi, T.S. Eliot, and Mother Teresa, we call wise. This is because they help us see beyond our immediate horizons, help us to frame our morality on more than our immediate short range interests, values, and readily grasped facts.

Certainly the devout believe their religion presents more than a theme. That does not diminish the value of what religion can offer in the present moral crisis. The devout can offer their vision as the ultimate truth about our moral situation. We can respond to it as it is offered. Let the vision that can command our belief and set our moral direction prevail. What it contributes to our moral life is the test of its validity.

This is the realm of human moral potential. Some writers, for example, Goethe, see mankind as constantly striving, ever becoming, rather than fixed in reality. To this I would add the thought that it is in action striving for the highest experiences possible that mankind is best understood, striving in the most effective manner, that is, in cooperation with others and that means being moral. It is foregoing immediate satisfaction, controlling oneself, overcoming immediate desire, to attain a greater end. This is being focused, in control of our lives and not being controlled by them. All of this we undertake with the best that has been thought and said and done before us. Religion can help us do that better.

Notes

1. Exodus 20: 1-17, N I V.
2. Nathaniel Hawthorne, *The Scarlet Letter,* New York, Courage Literary Classics, 1991.
3. *Mildred Pierce,* dir. Michael Curtiz, perf.. Joan Crawford, Zachary Scott, Ann Blyth, Bruce Bennett, Eve Arden, Warners, 1945.

Chapter V

ဣဩ

Ethics and Law: Collision Avoidance

"And always the loud angry crowd
Very angry and very loud
Law is We . . ."—W.H. Auden

As the moral authority of religion has eroded, people have turned to law as a source of morality. In the mind of many modernists there is little, if any, difference between law and morality. For some of these the only morality is in not getting caught breaking the law. There are dangers in taking law for morality, and the most serious is thinking that if something is legal, it is morally right. When that happens, law becomes an independent force governing our lives, and is amenable only to the changes required by law. A legal decision or a statute is what a judge or legislative body thinks it is. What is right is determined by the legislative process or the judicial process. Moral positions become justified or, at least, required by judicial or legislative activism. Such was the case with the prohibition of alcohol in the United States, and such is the case with the practice of abortion today.

Law and morality are intimately related, but the two are not identical. Black Americans experienced a pervasive legalized segregation largely social, economic and political. After Reconstruction, Southern states enacted laws prohibiting blacks from using public schools, hotels, restaurants, and public transportation. In 1896 the United States Supreme Court held such laws satisfied the equal protection clause of the fourteenth amendment of the Constitution through the doctrine of "separate but equal" in *Plessy v. Ferguson*.[1] The Fourteenth Amendment guarantees that no one person or group of persons be denied protection under law enjoyed by similar persons or groups. In short, similarly situated persons must receive similar treatment. Laws must be applied equally in all like cases. It also prohibits states from denying anyone "equal protection of the laws."

The segregation laws were intended to bring about two separate societies—one white and one black—and practically did. There were separate railroad cars, drinking fountains, schools, and, cemeteries. Separate residential areas, once the result of these laws, are still evident today. The theory was that all segregated arrangements would be separate but equal. In reality they were separate and very unequal. By restricting the meaning of the amendment to legal and political equality and ignoring social equality, the Supreme Court was able to uphold segregation. It even pointed to the existence of segregated schools as evidence that "equal protection" never meant desegregation. It is fallacious, the Court argued, to assume "that the enforced separation of the two races stamps the colored race with a badge of inferiority." It is also fallacious, the Court continued, to assume "that social prejudices may be overcome by legislation, and that equal rights cannot be secured to the Negro except by an enforced commingling of the two races." Social equality, the Court reasoned, "must be the result of natural affinities, a mutual appreciation of each other's merits, and a voluntary consent of individuals."

Not until nearly sixty years later did the United States Supreme Court rule in the landmark case, *Brown v. Board of Education of Topeka*, that racial segregation in public schools violated the Fourteenth Amendment to the Constitution.[2] The Court held that separate educational facilities were inherently unequal. Although this 1954 decision was limited to public schools, it was widely believed to imply that segregation in other public facilities was unconstitutional. While there were numerous individuals during the *Plessy v. Ferguson* years who claimed segregation was immoral, the Supreme Court did not find it was unconstitutional. Also while there were numerous individuals during the *Plessy v. Ferguson* years who saw nothing immoral in legal segregation, the Supreme Court did not rely on their moral grounds either. It relied on the following interpretation of the Fourteenth Amendment: "The object of the amendment was undoubtedly to enforce the absolute equality of the two races before the law, but, in the nature of things, it could not have been intended to abolish distinctions based upon color, or to enforce social, as distinguished from political, equality, or a commingling of the two races upon terms unsatisfactory to either."

There are numerous restraints on how a court resolves the issues before it. One of these is the cause itself, what the parties bring before the court. Another is the arguments the parties use and evidence they offer in support of their positions. Then there is the precedent set by comparable cases already decided in the Supreme Court, in other federal courts, and even in the state courts. There are the state constitutions and there is the U.S. Constitution itself and its amendments. There is seldom room for the judge's own moral view, but it does sometimes enter into how a judge decides an issue. It may not be explicitly stated as a moral view and probably will not be, but it can be recognized for what it is, though seldom is, even when the law affects morality.

In *Brown v. Board of Education*, the moral content is couched in sociological and psychological terms. Finding evidence that black and white schools involved have been equalized, or are being equalized, with regard to buildings, curricula, qualifications and salaries of teachers, and other tangible factors, the Court believed its decision had to turn on the effect of segregation itself on public education. "We must consider public education in the light of its full development and its present place in American life throughout the Nation." The Court found that education today ". . . is a principal instrument in awakening the child to cultural values, in preparing him for later professional training, and in helping him to adjust normally to his environment."

So the Court believed the question to be answered was this: "Does segregation of children in public schools solely on the basis of race, even though the physical facilities and other 'tangible' factors may be equal, deprive the children of the minority group of equal educational opportunities?" The Court concluded that it does.

Then the Court quotes from the decision in *McLaurin v. Oklahoma Board of Regents*:

> Segregation of white and colored children in public schools has a detrimental effect upon the colored children. The impact is greater

when it has the sanction of the law; for the policy of separating the races is usually interpreted as denoting the inferiority of the Negro group. A sense of inferiority affects the motivation of a child to learn. Segregation with the sanction of law, therefore, has a tendency to [retard] the educational and mental development of Negro children and to deprive them of some of the benefits they would receive in a racial [ly] integrated school system.[3]

The Court concludes that in the field of public education the doctrine of "separate but equal" has no place because separate educational facilities are inherently unequal. The plaintiffs and others similarly situated are by reason of the segregation they have complained of deprived of the equal protection of the laws guaranteed by the Fourteenth Amendment. In other words, if we take into account the abstract qualities of what makes for a really good education, we see that they cannot be present in minority schools because of the very facts that the Court felt in the *Plessy v. Ferguson* decision were irrelevant. A full philosophical analysis of this reasoning would require a special chapter, so I shall restrict the discussion to questions that help separate ethics from law.

First, can it really be conclusively determined that black schools cannot provide a top quality education, or that any student who goes to one will necessarily feel inferior? This seems at least doubtful despite the lavish testimony offered in support at the time. It is especially doubtful in light of the position being taken by contemporary minority leaders to end school bussing and for the maintenance of separate black colleges because they are supposed to be especially helpful to the development of confidence for black students. The Court opinion sometimes reads that there is an implied goal of bringing black students into the mainstream of education and values of the majority culture, something especially challenged today by advocates of multiculturalism.

The point here is not to cavil at the sociological and psychological "evidence" offered in support of the Court's decision. The decision was doubtless the right decision for the United States, especially in light of the subsequent rejection of the notion of "separate but equal" in virtually all other aspects of American life. The point, rather, is to marvel that the Supreme Court of the United States would hinge such a far reaching and beneficial decision on empirical evidence and not on the Constitution. From our vantage point today when it is clearly settled that segregation is insupportable, it seems strange that the Supreme Court did not just say so. But it had to deal with the legal restraint that when the Fourteenth Amendment was adopted, segregation was left completely in tact. In other words *Plessy v. Ferguson* held that we can have equal protection and segregation, too. That, after all, seemed consistent with what the framers of the Fourteenth Amendment intended.

The *Brown v. Board of Education* court found itself faced with the prospect of a flood of separate but equal cases and had to find a way to end them. It said segregated public schools were inherently unequal and states, therefore, could not allow their existence. That this was a practical solution was clear from the extension of the decision in *Brown v. Board of Education*, about segregated schools being inherently unequal, to public beaches, lunch counters, and a host of other then segregated public facilities. No attempt was made to show these were inherently unequal.

The notion "equal protection of the laws" was once thought general enough to be compatible with segregation and now with desegregation. Well, times change, and so then do our court rulings. But what is the constitutional basis for this particular change? Nothing new was offered beyond the claim that segregated public schools were inherently unequal. The results of the decision had far reaching consequences, too far reaching for their implied rationale.

But there is a moral basis in the Constitution for those who care to look for it: the moral ideal of individual equality. If we are to pursue the ideal of equality, then we must abandon the practice of segregation based on race. What had changed in the years since *Plessy v. Ferguson* was that undesirable consequences of segregation had unfolded. It was no longer possible to say it didn't matter that one race was being made to feel inferior to the other. But the moral ideal of individual equality had always been in the Constitution. It is a wonder the Court did not rely on it in its decision. Indeed, Supreme Court Justice Harlan who wrote the one dissenting opinion in *Plessy v. Ferguson* penned these words:

> . . . I deny that any legislative body or judicial tribunal may have regard to the race of citizens when the civil rights of those citizens are involved. Indeed, such legislation as that here in question is inconsistent not only with that equality of rights which pertains to citizenship, national and state, but with the personal liberty enjoyed by every one within the United States. . . .

And then he writes these splendid words:

... in view of the constitution, in the eye of the law, there is in this country no superior, dominant, ruling class of citizens. There is no caste here. Our constitution is color-blind, and neither knows nor tolerates classes among citizens. In respect of civil rights, all citizens are equal before the law. The humblest is the peer of the most powerful.

The moral ideal is present in the Constitution, but it did not have to be. Someone put it there. Whoever it was may not have been aware of its full implications, but those who followed were. That marks the principal relationship between law and morality: without the driving force of moral concepts, law is rudderless.

Before turning to a broader and more systematic comparison of law and morality, I want to make another observation that might be more readily grasped in this context than some others. We do not always see what is right or wrong, even though it is knowable to us, as here with the implications for segregation by the constitutional ideal of equality. This does not mean we are merely changing our minds when we do realize the implications, or that we are just swaying from one opinion to the other. It just means that we don't see it; we have a moral blindness. It may take a new situation such as historical change. It may take a new or perhaps overwhelming emotional experience such as a family crisis. At last we see how wrong we were and wonder how we could have missed the "truth" for so long. We often say "I was blind to the truth," or "I didn't want to face the truth." To be sure this is not justification for what we now say is the truth. That is another matter. All I am saying here is that we can be blind to the actions our moral convictions require of us. Martin Luther King, Jr. dedicated his life to the proposition that those who supported segregation would see it as unjust if once he was able to open their moral eyes.

Law will only be as good as the morality it expresses, but, without the enactment and enforcement of law, social life, the substance of morality, is practically impossible as long as human beings are made the way they are and continue to behave accordingly. So it is practically impossible to say whether law or morality comes first, either in time or logic. Thomas Hobbes saw morality and law as identical in the sense that the establishment of government was the entire basis of social order and there was no morality until a system of laws was in effect. Indeed, for Hobbes it is law that provides the stability required for social life.[4] This seems to be true for Plato as well. Law is the backbone of society, so to speak.[5]

In addition, there are features of law that reflect or parallel morality. Law and morality both have appealed to authority for justification. For some, law is an expression of God's will which is dominant over all creatures, especially human beings. And so our laws, to the extent they are just, are decreed by God and rest on Gods authority. The most familiar example of this is the so-called "divine right of kings." The notion is that a king governs by virtue of being ordained on his throne by God.

Other thinkers have claimed law is "given" by the natural order of the universe. Law is not the result of mere human effort although it is detectable by human reason. Law is not my idea or your idea but based in reality. So it is not for us to decide to follow the law. The law is given by nature, and those who do not follow the law are going against nature. The most familiar example of this kind of thinking is the notion of justice. "An eye for an eye, and a tooth for a tooth" as expressed in the code of Hammurabi implies the belief that there is a balance in nature to be restored after a crime. The balance is restored by the infliction of a penalty that "fits" the crime. The criminal gets what he deserves as the result of his action.

Still others, perhaps more cynical thinkers, have claimed the source of law is merely the will of the dominant person or class in society. This thinking is illustrated in modern dictatorship. The strong person lays down the law, and the people follow it because it is the will of the person who has the power to make all others obey him. Thus, his word is law. There may also be a class who rule the others by virtue of some special status. They may have land holdings or other wealth or be descendants of certain people recognized by the others as authorized to rule them. They are the aristocrats. In a democratic society, though, the people elect officials to make laws for them. In this way the authority of the laws passed by the elected officials theoretically lies in its being the will of the people as they have expressed it in their votes.

Law has also been said to be based on its own authority, that is its efficacy in resolving conflicts of interest (render justice) and in directing human action into proper courses. Here, again the validity of the laws is based, not on men, but in the systematic resolution of conflicts while recognizing individual rights and interests and coordinating the activities of the members of the society in productive ways.

Also, law is an appealing morality substitute in a variety of ways. Law frequently incorporates the collective, funded experience of a people and puts it to use. Law tends to be impartial and generalizable and so protects the individual, and it serves as a check on personal impulse, lays out limits for rights and privileges. It lays out what is expected of us and gives clear penalties for violations. It should anyway. It keeps us mindful of the objective features of human association—the claims and rights of others and need to make truthful, factual arguments in advocating our interests and rights against those of others. Like morality, law purports to be impersonal and impartial, engendering the respect needed for social order.

After the preceding reflections on these features of law, we can see why people tend to confuse law with morality. But the two are not the same. Law and morality are typically grounded on some kind of authority and in that they are similar, but the authority each ultimately rests upon is not the same. Failure to distinguish them contributes to the loss of ethical sense in modern societies. Ideally the two provide mutual support for each other.

It is often said, "You can't legislate morality." This statement, taken alone, implies too much separation between law and morality. Practically everyone holds that murder, taking the life of another human being without justification, is morally wrong. The same is true for sexual violence. Yet all civilized societies also have laws dealing with murder and rape. It is clear, then, that we do sometimes legislate morality. Certain matters are so vital to social life that we want them in the form of law to employ the force of law in assuring certain social behavior. The kernel of wisdom contained in the saying about legislating morality is not that moral requirements cannot be made into law because they can be. It is, rather, that just because they are enacted into law does not mean people will obey them if they don't really think they should.

There are problems of legally enforcing certain moral practices. For example, there are promises we make to one another which the law will not enforce. One law school definition of a contract is a promise which the courts will enforce. In fact, according to the English common law the courts presumed the parties did not intend to be legally bound when a husband and wife living together on friendly terms made an agreement. In one case, there was evidence the parties even stated they intended their agreement to be legally binding. But as a matter of "public policy," a legal term of art, about half of the courts refused to enforce such agreements lest they be flooded with actions. They also feared suits of that nature would interfere with internal family harmony.

In an English case in 1919, *Balfour v. Balfour*, the court said a wife could not recover damages even though her husband promised her an allowance of 30 pounds sterling a month. The court based its decision on the ground that ". . . it would be of the worst possible example to hold that agreements such as this resulted in legal obligations which could be enforced in the Courts. In respect of these promises each house is a domain into which the King's writ does not seek to run, and to which his officers do not seek to be admitted."[6]

A fundamental moral practice, promise making between husband and wife, was not a concern of the courts when it came to domestic matters because of the problems of managing all of the cases. Today the law is changing in this regard and more agreements between husband and wife are finding court sanction. This seems especially true where a husband wife joint commercial undertaking is involved. But, wherever the law has been or is now going, it would be an error to infer from any of this that morality does not hold husbands and wives to their promises to one another.

On January 29, 1920 the Prohibition Amendment to the United States Constitution went into effect. It was the Eighteenth Amendment. The intention was to prevent the manufacture, sale, and transportation of alcoholic beverages and effect abstinence by means of law. For over a decade the federal government enforced prohibition in varying degrees. Prohibition was enforceable where the population was sympathetic to it and not where the population was not sympathetic. Historically, this meant it was enforced in small towns and rural areas but not in large cities. Eventually, even the major prohibitionists began to realize legal enforcement was virtually impossible when the speakeasies flourished and the illegal manufacture and sale of liquor increased. On December 5, 1933 the Twenty-first Amendment to the Constitution repealing prohibition went into effect.

The story of prohibition teaches us several lessons about the difference between law and morality. For one, it is virtually impossible to uphold a law when large numbers of the people affected by the law do not agree with it. To expect people to follow the law is to expect them to do it on the basis of their belief in the moral rectitude of the law. For another, the law can be enforced only when the majority of the citizens support it, and then the few who do not can be compelled to follow it by the use of governmental power. It is practically impossible to enact and uphold laws unless they are seen by the people as in their interest. Usually laws are enacted to assure that the most serious moral precepts and those most difficult to maintain through moral sanction alone are followed.

Some of our morality is best put into law because the legal institutions can make it clear who does the enforcing and what the specific costs of disobedience are. This is in contrast to moral sanctions which may be vague as to the enforcer and the consequences of disobedience. Also, we require some laws to make us do what we are not likely to do or not do what we are likely to do but shouldn't.

Law and morality may be thought of as two overlapping circles. Where they overlap we have what we may regard as just and enforceable laws. They do not overlap in two places. The first is where laws are without moral footing, what we call unjust laws, as the Jim Crow laws were found to be. The second is where morality is not enacted, perhaps not enactable, into law.

In the law of torts the distinction between liability for action and liability for inaction provides us another significant point of contrast between law and morality. It also provides a look at the way law changes in relation to morality. Early in the formation of the English common law, a person who injured another by something he did was liable for that injury, and it did not matter very much whether the person was morally at fault for the injury. In contrast, the common law tended not to be concerned with the person who, by not acting when he could have, allowed another to receive injury. This, according to Prosser, was because the courts were too much occupied with flagrant misbehavior.[7] As a result, the law developed a deep separation between misfeasance and nonfeasance.

In other words, the law made a distinction between actively producing positive injury and passively not protecting another from injury. By the former one "creates a new risk of harm" to another. By the latter one has "at least made his [another's] situation no worse, and has merely failed to benefit him by interfering in his affairs."[8] Prosser provides a revealing comment on this distinction:

> The highly individualistic philosophy of the older common law had no great difficulty in working out restraints upon the commission of affirmative acts of harm, but shrank from converting the courts into an agency for forcing men to help one another.[9]

What is wrong with converting the courts into an agency for forcing men to help one another? The courts have made it their business to see to it that people do not interfere with the affairs of one another. Keeping people from interfering with one another is a more manageable task than directing people in helping one another. But it is just this business of helping one another that is the essence of morality. Helping one another is engaging in social purpose.

The "separate but equal" court comes to mind here. To be sure, this is constitutional and not tort law, but in ruling the court was reluctant to tell people they had to be together socially, even though the court could read the Fourteenth Amendment in no other way than that each individual was equal before the law and couldn't really be equal if there are places in his life where he cannot go for the benefits of society. It had to insist that civil rights be preserved, but it was averse to forcing people to interact together socially and left it to people to do voluntarily. That, too, is part of morality—voluntary cooperation among individuals. This would include the mutual expectation of assistance in time of need. Separate societies would all but preclude this.

Because the law is reluctant to hold one liable for what he does not do it does not obligate a stranger to aid another human being in danger, even of losing his life. Yet one would be hard pressed to find a society whose members did not feel morally obligated to help one another especially in peril. Just how significant this difference between the common law and morality is comes home in some amazing legal decisions.

In one case, *Osterlind v. Hill*, the defendant, an expert swimmer who had with him a boat and a rope and had even rented a canoe to the intoxicated plaintiff who capsized it, was not required by law to do anything as he saw the man drowning before him.[10] An even more shocking decision is found in *Yania v. Bigan*.[11] Here the plaintiff was even a business visitor. The defendant encouraged him to jump in the water, and when the plaintiff was unable to swim, he let him drown offering no assistance. Prosser comments on these cases as follows:

> A physician is under no duty to answer the call of one who is dying and might be saved, nor is anyone required to play the part of Florence Nightengale and bind up the wounds of a stranger who is bleeding to death, or to prevent a neighbor's child from hammering on a dangerous explosive, or to remove a stone from a highway where it is a menace to traffic, or a train from a place where it blocks a fire engine on its way to save a house, or even to cry a warning to one who is walking into the jaws of a dangerous machine.[12]

The point is not to cast the law as morally unworthy, but to show the law is different from morality. Many legal writers have deplored these decisions as morally offensive. But so far the law has not been able to establish a general standard for judging what service to one's fellow humans should be required, just how far one has to go out of his way to help another. The law has been gradually finding duties to others created by special relationships among individuals. Apart from such relationships the law leaves the remedy in such cases to the "higher law" and the "voice of conscience," or, in other words, to morality.

We can expect continuing pressure on the law to develop such a standard, but until it does, we should bear in mind the two overlapping circles. We have just seen one more area where the circle of morality is not overlapped by law. But we should also observe that the line between morality and law can be expected to change, as we are able and decide to put more morality into law. As our social experience unfolds our knowledge expands, our moral thinking may become clearer and, as a result, we may modify our laws. This was apparent in our brief reflection on segregation in the United States. The full meaning of equality was not recognized by the majority of the Court until the consequences of separate classes of citizens unfolded. We enact laws to produce moral results, and we repeal laws when we no longer desire their moral results or when they do not have the moral results we anticipated at enactment, or when, as in the case of "separate but equal" our moral perception improves.

Some law does not even bear directly on morality. For example, it does not matter whether we drive on the right or on the left side of the street, but to have orderly flow of traffic it must be one or the other. This part of law may be termed "administrative" in contrast to law with direct moral bearing. To be sure, one who flouts even administrative law does moral wrong because respect for the laws of one's community is a moral expectation. But in contrast with law that has direct moral bearing, as does that pertaining to vice, say, there is a difference. Administrative law is law we follow just because it is the law. There is no moral driving force behind it. There are those who think of all law in that way. For them, all that matters is that they have laws to suit them. For example, if you can get a Supreme Court decision that it is unconstitutional to ban abortion, then you have eliminated abortion as a moral issue.

The error in identifying law and morality should be clear by now, but in case it isn't it can be made even clearer with reflections on the ethical dilemma presented by Kenneth Blanchard and Norman Vincent Peale.

Sales had been down for almost six months and my boss was putting pressure on me to get my division's numbers up. I'd been involved for a month in a search for a topflight experienced sales representative to add to my sales force, and three days ago I had interviewed a very likely prospect.

From the moment he walked confidently into my office, I'd felt this man was just the person I needed. As the interview proceeded I became more and more excited. It was obvious that I'd be lucky to get this person. He had an outstanding sales record and knew our industry backward and forward. Most intriguingly, he had just quit a top job with our major competitor, after six successful years with that company.

. . . I'd just about made up my mind to hire him . . . when he smiled, reached into his attache case, and pulled out a small, square envelope. From it he extracted a computer disc, and held it up as if it were a priceless gem.

"Can you guess what's on this disc?" he said

I shook my head.

Still smiling, his voice oozing with self-assurance, he proceeded to explain that the disc contained a wealth of confidential information about our competitor, his former employer—including profiles of all their customers and cost data on a major defense-contract bid for which our company was also competing. As we closed out the interview session, he promised me that, if I hired him, he would give me this disc and more of the same.[13]

The dilemma is whether it is right or wrong to hire this person. A well trained manager would be alert to the legal risks involved and would be sure to seek legal counsel on the matter. This would be an almost automatic response. There are laws dealing with trade secrets and inside information, and the penalties are serious. The prudent manager will be very careful here. But the law itself is changing. Certainly the case law is, and it is not certain where either the manager or the applicant would be at the end of a suit for breach of contract not to divulge trade secrets brought by the applicant's former employer. So, what should be the guide? Would it be "wise" to hire the applicant?

As Blanchard and Peale explain, even if either or both are lucky in the law, the two of them will be compromised in their own eyes, and in the eyes of anyone who will know about it. That diminishes prospects for good working relationships. They would hardly be able to trust each other knowing that each had participated in deceiving the applicant's former employer. Anyone else at the manager's company who knew about the deception would hardly be able to trust them. If they did that to the former employer, they might well do it to their current employer when it suited them. Moreover, neither they nor the company who condones their action can expect to hold the esteem of other companies, in the same trade certainly and probably in any other trade. This means impaired business relations. Using the law alone as a guide to what is right is risking a great deal.

These considerations, however, are basically material, not moral. There is a difference between not doing something that is against the law because you might get caught and not doing it because it is wrong. There is also a difference in not doing something because it doesn't pay or because it might cost you something personally and not doing it because it is wrong. In the language of ethics, this is called the difference between prudence and morality—looking out for yourself and doing what is right. Sometimes they are the same; sometimes not. Just because something is in your interest does not mean it is not moral. It may be in your interest to visit Aunt Tillie because she has no direct heirs and may leave you her estate, but it may also be the right thing to do because she is lonesome. On the other hand, just because something is in your interest does not mean it is right to pursue it.

It is in my interest to take the one thousand dollars I need for clothes to get a good job from the old timer living alone in the country house where I stopped for water for my car. The old timer is blind, extremely absent minded, has no telephone, and is miles from any help. He has far more money in an open cash box than the one thousand I am planning to slip from it unbeknownst to him. He doesn't even know I am in the house. It is certain I can take the money, get the clothes and the good job, become a productive citizen, even give money to charity when I am earning as I am not now, never be found out by the law, and never cause any real hardship for the old timer. So as far as the law is concerned, I am safe. There is no way I will be apprehended. As far as my conscience tells me, my plan is going to serve my interest, possibly the interest of others when I give to charity, and not harm anyone in the process.

Should I take the money and, in doing so, break the law? I know I can "get away" with it. There is always the remote possibility I might be caught, but it is as certain as anything can ever be that I will not. Still, most people would feel that there is something not right about this, even though they may not be able to say just what. What is missing is the general social interest in respect for private property. It furthers our social purpose to inculcate an attitude of respect for private property. We don't have to keep looking over our shoulder to see who is trying to take stuff from us that we were planning to use for some long range purpose and accomplish more with it than we would if we expended it all right on the spot. Because it is so important to have this we pass laws to help safeguard it. But, as we have seen, law can only do so much to protect it.

Now we can look back at the manager and applicant. They can calculate it is in their interest and they probably can get away with pirating the former employer's trade secrets. They know the business risks such as losing respect of their colleagues and possibly other companies if they are discovered. On the plus side of being found out they could even be admired for trying such a bold measure. So, as any reasonable people and just as I with the old timer's money, they calculate that it is worth taking the risk of hiring the applicant and using his computer disc with the chief competitor's secret data to make a big score for themselves and the company. They have, essentially, bracketed the law because they have decided they will not get caught, and they have estimated that the business consequences of being discovered would be relatively minor for them. As for their own estimation of one another for being dishonest, they swear to each other that they will never tell anyone and they are "in this together." They go ahead with their plan, and they succeed. The company recovers. The two men are promoted for their sharp ideas, the former employer experiences only a short term drop in the rate of increase of sales, and everyone lives happily ever after.

Here is where Hollywood morality, where the crooks are romanticized as clever, great looking lovers and don't do any "real" harm, thrives. But real morality must condemn the action because what the two did was a disservice to each and every one of us. As a society it is our purpose to support manufacturing and commerce because doing so benefits all of us. At least, that is our intention. When these activities are distorted for personal gain, we have been betrayed, not that personal gain is out of place in business, quite the contrary, but if individuals are allowed to use deceptive practices for personal gain, business itself is jeopardized and this thwarts our common purpose. It makes it that much harder to work together.

If the social expectation were that any one or two people should decide when they would keep their promises to employers and when they would not, when they would resort to deceptive practices in conducting their affairs and when they would not, it would be impossible to trust employees and managers and, eventually impossible to do business at all. That would be material harm, but it would also be moral harm because the entire society is debilitated by having corrupt business operations and so unable to further itself. It could not rely on business to do it, and would have to resort to some other way. But try to imagine what a society would be like that could not have sound commercial enterprise. A few people can cheat and get away with it, and the society can tolerate it for a while but not when it becomes widespread. So in the absence of being able to say just when, how far, and for whom such deceptive practices can be tolerated, morality requires that no one engages in them.

This is not to say morality will make everyone honest. It is only to say there is a moral reason why people have to be honest. Society misses its boat by not training people to be honest, and the main reason it does not today is that the members of society do not understand the preceding reasoning. Why people will want to be moral will be discussed later, but it should suffice here to say that being moral is the price we each have to pay for the cooperation society provides and its resulting benefits to us.

Returning to law and morality, there are two reasons to obey the law. One is that we might be caught. But that is a reason of self-interest. There is another reason, a moral reason: it is right to obey the law because it promotes a stronger society. And here we see the fundamental difference between law and morality. When and where law does not contribute to the strength of a society, it no longer furthers moral purpose, and is in fact no longer just law. The error of identifying law and morality obscures the moral question. This is why those who cannot dominate the morality of a society attempt to have their way by controlling the enactment of laws and the decisions of courts. This is also why people who want to be moral but do not understand that morality and law are different are struck dumb when there is a law or a legal decision made contrary to what they believe makes for a strong society. If they recognize the difference, they can well work independently to enforce the morality being plowed under by those who would control and manipulate the law.

Here the matter of civil disobedience arises. When is it right to disobey because you believe the law is immoral or, as is commonly said, an unjust law? This is a complex question requiring an elaborate discussion which may not prove conclusive. It must be laid aside, but two comments may be in order. First, if there were no difference between law and morality, the question of civil disobedience could never arise. Second, over the centuries those who have chosen to disobey what they believed were unjust laws have usually been willing to undergo the penalties for disobeying the laws. In doing so they have shown both respect for law, as a social institution, and their objection to a particular law. Also, in doing so they have hoped to appeal to the conscience of society to see the immorality of the law they were protesting. Typically, Mahatma Ghandi and Martin Luther King, Jr. hoped their disobedience and willingness to suffer the penalty would dramatize the injustice of the laws they found unfair. They appealed to the morality of their oppressors. They could not do this if morality were that same as their law.

Because law and morality are not the same we can expect they will not always be in harmony. Historically, law and morality have changed as the result of a multiplicity of factors. Political factors, new information, and new situations affect law. Changing perceptions, new information, and new situations affect morality. This is no wonder. People are constantly trying to cast both according to their own beliefs. That is the heart of the problem of ethics in contemporary society—finding a basis of universal appeal, a moral authority, we can all obey.

Traditionally, murder, fornication, divorce, homosexuality, abortion, suicide, and euthanasia were morally forbidden in Western societies, and laws were enacted against them and other morally forbidden acts regarded as equally serious. There are still many people in these societies today who believe the laws against these acts should be strictly enforced, and there are now many people who believe they should not. At present, we are all having difficulty enforcing the laws, and much of this is caused by changes in moral beliefs. Taking abortion as one example, in the United States there is essentially a compromise between warring factions in the Supreme Court decision *Row v. Wade*.[14] The Court found a right to privacy in the Constitution and this somehow allows a woman to decide to terminate her pregnancy through the end of the first trimester. It is not evident why the right ends at the first trimester, but it appears to be based on a few nineteenth century court decisions. These decisions were made when the mistaken belief was that there was no life in the womb until the fetus started moving, usually after three months.

Without getting into the complex reasoning of the Court, it is fair to say it was decided as a matter of individual rights balanced against the interest of state governments in regulating pregnancy from the standpoint of the health of the expectant woman and, after three months, the unborn child. No regard is or could be given to the moral interest of the society because to do so would be to depart from strictly legal and in this case constitutional matters and to impose the moral opinion of the justices. To do so would be to raise questions about the entire society's interest in who is having babies and who is not and why not and what does that bode for the future of the society in light of how we are tending to the successor generation. The ramifications are many. Who raises the children who are not aborted? What happens if everyone decides to have an abortion, or decides to abort female fetuses? Who looks after the older generation if there are not enough babies being born? Can the society protect itself against the vicissitudes of fortune without requiring those of child bearing age to make decisions about children with the welfare of the whole society in mind?

Similar questions have to be asked about the other traditionally forbidden practices. What bearing do they have on the social purpose? Does the moral community miss a serious opportunity for furthering the security of all by categorically condemning homosexuality and not asking whether homosexuals strengthen the society by their presence? To be sure, this is fraught with anxious questions, but possibly with the right supporting structures, our futures might be enhanced instead of preoccupied with repressing some of our members. Of course, it might turn out to be the opposite. Open tolerance or encouragement of homosexuality may be found to detract from marriage and other valued social institutions. In that case the opposite may be our moral conclusion. These are questions and not answers, but they do present the manner by which a moral community can go about resolving these moral questions and enact laws accordingly.

There are always questions about minorities, and the rationale for morality offered in this book is bound to make these questions strongly felt. Are we to suppress individuals and groups for the greater good? Even if we acknowledge that some of this must be done from time to time, how far do we go in doing so? Where is the line between coordinating behavior and repressing behavior, and should we acknowledge it? Because morality, as we have seen, is based on voluntary participation there can be no doubt that the line must be acknowledged; otherwise, we have some people dominating others. But just because we must acknowledge the line exists does not mean that it is always easy to draw.

Some reflections on another court case will be helpful here. This is a case brought before the Supreme Court of the State of New Jersey. JFK Memorial Hospital administered a blood transfusion to save the life of a young woman, Delores Heston, age 22, who tried to refuse the transfusion for religious reasons. The case has many implications for individual freedom, but I will focus on just the ones raised in the preceding paragraph. Miss Heston, presumably not being able to opt for or against a release, the hospital applied to a judge of the superior court for the appointment of a guardian for Miss Heston with directions to consent to transfusions as needed to save her life. The court did so, surgery was performed at 4:00 A.M. the same morning, blood was given, and Miss Heston survived.

Later, Miss Heston appealed the superior court's order to the New Jersey Supreme Court. Even though that court felt the matter moot, it decided to rule because of strong public interest in the matter. After exploring a number of precedent cases on related issues including the individual's rights to die and to commit suicide, the court affirmed the lower courts decision allowing the hospital to perform the transfusions: "We find that the interest of the hospital and its staff, as well as the State's interest in life, warranted the transfusion of blood under the circumstances of this case." Notice the phrase, "interest in life." This is what I have been saying is the ultimate social purpose from which decisions of right and wrong derive. The protection of our lives is our greatest assurance of our individual liberty. Look closely at the reasoning of the court.

> Hospitals exist to aid the sick and the injured. The medical and nursing professions are consecrated to preserving life. That is their professional creed. To them, a failure to use a simple, established procedure in the circumstances of this case would be malpractice, however the law may characterize that failure because of the patient's private convictions. A surgeon should not be asked to operate under the strain of knowing that a transfusion may not be administered even though medically required to save this patient. The hospital and its staff should not be required to decide whether the patient is or continues to be competent to make a judgment upon the subject, or whether the release tendered by the patient or a member of his family will protect them from civil responsibility. The hospital could hardly avoid the problem by compelling the removal of a dying patient, and Miss Heston's family made no effort to take her elsewhere.

When the hospital and staff are thus involuntary hosts and their interests are pitted against the belief of the patient, we think it reasonable to resolve the problem by permitting the hospital and its staff to pursue their functions according to their professional standards.[15]

In a pluralistic society, as most modern countries are, we have difficulty finding closure on moral issues, except when it matters. When it does, we find that coming down on the side that protects life the best way we know how yields the answer to the question, "What is right?" That is because the entire community is premised on the protection of life. It should not be surprising that hospitals, their staffs, and physicians should be dedicated to that, and that the laws would protect their work. That is consistent with our social purpose. Our society is organized to protect our lives. So, too, are our other institutions and our social expectations of one another.

We can see also that the right to religious freedom exists only when it does not matter to the social purpose. This is also true for all of the other rights we are so fond of cultivating in modern democratic countries. When these rights in practice interfere with the basic reasons we, as individuals, have voluntarily joined together in the first place, they are often abridged. Think of what would happen to the right to personal freedom should one of these countries feel it was necessary to conscript individuals into an army for national defense.

The point is not to make light of individual rights, but only to remind us that they depend on social purpose. Assuring individual rights makes for a more productive society. When and where it does not, the rights can be and often are abridged. The pulling apart we are experiencing in modern societies throughout the world results from failure to recognize why there are societies in the first place. Societal protection of life makes our freedom possible. When we recall the reason clearly, we shape our laws accordingly just as the members of the New Jersey Supreme Court did.

And this provides a guide to how we will be able to resolve the other controversial moral matters mentioned earlier. Can we tolerate unbridled sexual freedom and remain a coherent society? Can we allow each person total freedom over his life and expect no implications for the rest of us in society? And if we cannot, then what are the limits? They will be those imposed by the reality of pursuing the benefits of moral community, that is, we limit them when we cannot get on with the business of working together for the protection and promotion of our lives.

When we cannot expect these limits to be self-imposed, we pass laws and make legal decisions to enforce them. The New Jersey justices did not appeal to a specific moral authority in making their decision. That might make one think they were not thinking morally. But they were. Indeed, they were doing profound moral thinking. They made their decision on the basis of the moral principle that is so fundamental that they did not even realize it was moral: our societies and their institutions, when properly governed are established for the protection of life and the promotion of civilization.

When law functions properly, it furthers our moral purpose, and that is the promotion and protection of the freedom of individuals consistent with the freedom of every other individual in the society. Law and morality must be distinguished in order for us to be able to tell when law is functioning properly. Otherwise, we would still be in the Jim Crow era or something worse.

Having distinguished law and morality, though recognizing they are always and to our benefit intertwined, it is time to turn to government and morality to see if a comparable distinction between government and morality might be useful in clarifying some of the moral confusion we sense in our time.

Notes

1. 163 U.S. 537 (1896)
2. 347 U.S. 483 (1954)
3. 339 U.S. 637 (1950)
4. See Chapter III, Section 1 above.
5. Laws, Book XII.
6. 2 K.B. 571 (C.A.)
7. *Prosser and Keeton on Torts,* fifth edition, West Publishing Co., St. Paul, Minnesota, 1984, pp. 373ff.
8. *Ibid*, p 373
9. *Ibid*
10. 1928, 263 Mass;. 73, 160 N.E. 301
11. 1959, 397 Pa. 316, 155 A2d 343
12. *op. cit.*, p. 375
13. Kenneth Blanchard & Norman Vincent Peale, *The Power of Ethical Management,* New York: William Morrow & Company, Inc. 1988, pp..11-12.
14. 410 U.S. 113 (1973)
15. *JFK Memorial Hospital v. Heston,* 58 N.J. 576 (1971)

Chapter VI

ॐ

Ethics, Government, and the Politically Correct: Navigational Aids and Obstacles

> "If politics in America is not to become the art of the
> impossible, the limits of politics must be perceived and the
> province of moral philosophy greatly expanded."
> —Senator Daniel Patrick Moynihan

During the 1996 United States presidential election the candidates and their friends often said the election was about values. Candidates spoke about "family values." Others even said the election was a battle for the "soul of America." Since this was an election, the debate implied a choice of values. If the American people elected the right political party, they could then proceed to implement the moral society of their choice. That is extremely hard to believe. In fact, it is so hard to believe, we can reasonably conclude that the realm of values is not coextensive with politics. Government is not coextensive with the totality of moral affairs of a society, especially one as complex as the United States.

This is not easy for the modernist to understand. Thomas Moore, in his best seller *The Care of the Soul*[1] uses the term "psychological modernism" and defines it as the uncritical acceptance of the values of the modern world, blind faith in technology, inordinate attachment to material gadgets and conveniences, uncritical acceptance of the march of scientific "progress," devotion to the electronic media, and a life style dictated by advertising. I would elicit from this cluster definition the dependence on government for the values of the modern world. And part of the blind faith in technology is the use of social engineering to fix any and all problems of group living.

The modernist cannot see the difference between government and morality. Government now affects so many areas of our life—health care, education, welfare, retirement, and safety. We have had the "Great Society," the "War on Poverty," the "War on Drugs," the "Education Presidency," and a host of other social fixes. We are even told government controls the economy, and the Supreme Court is the arbiter, if not the author, of American values. It is not surprising that many people, especially younger Americans, wait to see what government policy or court rulings are in order to decide what is right and what is wrong in their society.

If a nation designs its constitution and institutions properly, some of its most basic values should be embodied in them and guide the conduct of governmental affairs. It is worth noting, though, that even in the United States, whose government was designed directly to implement the moral ideals of individual equality and freedom, the ethical values are implied in the Bill of Rights, amendments to the original Constitution. The Constitution itself sets out the structure of government and not its moral purpose. So, we must be constantly vigilant to interpret the Constitution and the Bill of Rights according to our moral values.

Consider that the notion of equality of citizens was embedded in the Constitution, but only lately have we faced what that means for women and minorities and many would say we are still trying to get this right. This is because we as a people are trying to direct our government on these matters. We have not embodied the entirety of our moral beliefs in the government.

Despite this twentieth century preoccupation with government, we have begun to see that government has limitations when it comes to solving social problems and has even caused some problems of its own. We have three and four generations of families on welfare, a government program originally intended to help people in short term need. This was, no doubt a program of high moral intention, but it served political purposes to overextend it. The intention to use government to carry out a moral idea became a program of dubious moral worth considering what might have been for the families so long dependent on government.

To begin to make sense of this we have to reflect first on what exactly we mean by "government," and second on why, if at all, we need it. It comes almost as a surprise that the primary dictionary meaning of "government" is the "the process of ruling." The surprise is that the word refers to a process and not a thing. We are accustomed to referring to and thinking of the government as a body of people elected and sitting in offices and buildings and bureaus. We think, if at all, of government as a process only secondarily. But when we think of the process of ruling, we are led immediately to two observations: there are those who rule and there are those who are ruled.

How one distinguishes between the two has varied widely among the various peoples of the world. Rulers have been the single person autocrat. They have been a special class of people, an aristocracy. They have even been the people themselves, a democracy. But usually those who have ruled in a democracy were defined in some way as citizens and not merely the whole of the people who happen to be living in a certain area. Usually those who ruled were the majority of the citizens or representatives of the people chosen by the majority to govern. In any case the ruler governed by virtue of being especially qualified to do so.

By comparison, a society or a moral community, as defined in this book, is a body of people voluntarily joined by common purpose and carrying out their individual responsibilities to see that their shared purpose is fulfilled. No one governs because each person in the society performs voluntarily everything he is supposed to do. Debaters would quickly conclude that a moral community is not a governed community and a governed community is not a moral community. In the academic world they would be right. But in the real world community membership is never static, always dynamic. Babies are born into them, adults die out of them, and people come in and go out of them. One could hardly expect everyone either to know what is expected of him or willingly to carry out his duties.

Most communities do not have the benefit of their individual members doing everything they are supposed to do and, consequently, have to have a ruling authority, a government, to require them to do what they cannot be expected to do voluntarily. In addition, most communities have to structure governmental machinery to coordinate their members in actions requiring formal organization. In other words, most communities are not fully moral communities in the sense that people living within them are not fully prepared to act as moral agents, children, for example, and others not capable of shouldering the responsibilities imposed by the moral community. Even though these are simple and obvious truths, it is surprising how little preparation is given to children and newcomers for their social responsibilities.

Ordinarily communities will try to bring everyone into the moral circle, so to speak, and use government, a ruler in some form, to help by formally requiring those who do not cooperate to do so. They will also use government to create organizations—an army, a highway system, a postal service, a monetary system—that are best formally established and operated through government. Anyone who has raised children knows children are not capable of deciding for themselves what is best for themselves or others. Parents know it is always a demanding task to allow children just the right amount of responsibility they can handle and no more so they can begin to "grow up" and eventually become responsible adults capable of living on their own. Anyone who has lived in society as a responsible adult also knows that some people, no matter how old they are, are not and probably can never become morally responsible adults and for that reason must be governed by law.

Since there will never be a time when everyone in a community is fully adult or fully committed to the social purpose, there will always be the need for government. That is why it is naive to believe there should be a time when there will be no government or that the properly conceived society would need no government. It is not a matter of the best government being the government that governs least, but a matter of having as much government as is necessary given the stage of moral development of the community. Is is also not a matter of waiting until government is no longer necessary. Because any community lives in time it will always require the support of government. Also, because certain collective activities can be most effective when formalized through law and governmental apparatus there will be continuing need for government.

In our present day, however, we have allowed government to serve as a substitute for morality rather than an agent of it. In replacing some of the roles of morality government has had the effect of weakening morality. Where government has entered, organizations founded on ethical or religious foundations have exited. Hospitals, schools, and other charitable institutions have closed as no longer necessary or even possible because government is perceived as meeting the needs these organizations were founded to meet. The civil rights legislation of the 1960's has had the salutary effect of legally proscribing racial discrimination. But it may also have had the effect of canceling racial discrimination as a moral issue. By allowing government to become the moral arbiter rather than using government to carry out our moral objectives, we abdicate our moral responsibility.

One reason for this is the limitation of government as a moral agent. Without preserving moral rationale and sanction and relying on government to define our social objectives, we are able to accomplish morally only what government can do. "You cannot legislate morality." This saying is partly true and partly false. It is false because you can get people to behave outwardly in a morally desirable manner when they are in fear of being apprehended and punished. It is true because people will try to get away with immoral conduct unless they believe in their hearts that such conduct is wrong. Since it is practically impossible to place the police at everyone's elbow, the law does little good where it cannot be enforced. Civil rights laws can be enacted and enforced in selected areas where violation can be detected and laws enforced, but this cannot stamp out racial prejudice. That means discrimination will rear its ugly head whenever it thinks it will go unapprehended or unpunished.

In August 1994 Texaco executives were recorded making racially offensive comments in a corporate office. In so doing, the executives were violating corporate conduct guidelines stating that "conduct directed toward any employee which is unwelcome, hostile, offensive, degrading or abusive is unacceptable and will not be tolerated."[2] The nature of the comments cast doubt on Texaco's good faith and led to substantial financial loss and embarrassment for the company. This happened despite company policy written in response to state and federal regulations and during a time when the company was being sued for unfair treatment of its minority employees.

Lehman Brothers analyst William Randol said "This is an isolated incident, which isn't at all reflected in Texaco's corporate policy."[3] So it may be and so an objective reader may conclude. The failure of one or two executives to observe policy, or even government regulations does not prove that government and corporate policy cannot be effective. But a closer look at the actual comments the two executives made shows they resented the policy because they did not morally accept the guidelines. The comments took place in private, behind the backs, of the other employees. This circumstance was particularly aggravating because it was evidence that these executives did not believe in the policy. The company could say what it found politically correct to say, but it employed at high levels individuals who could not be trusted.

The moral dimension of human relations is manifest at such moments. It is when people are not coerced into certain behavior that one can tell what they really believe. And it is in these private moments that we have to trust others to think and do what is morally right. No governmental or corporate action or decree can assure that individuals on their own will do what is right, but here is where we find the ultimate basis of human relations.

Still, governmental action is frequently necessary. Governmental intervention at the federal level in the United States was very likely necessary to dislodge deeply entrenched patterns of racial segregation and discrimination. These patterns would have continued in most of the United States without it. Intervention did help change outward behavior, and it even helped change attitudes. It has been reported that white lunch counter owners who wanted to serve blacks, both because it meant more business and because they thought it was the right thing to do, were afraid of losing their white customers if they did. With the formal imposition of governmental action, the owners could tell their white customers they had to serve blacks. This may even have furthered a moral result by permitting whites to see certain social benefits from the integration of the lunch counters. This is not to say some whites, even today, do not resent the presence of blacks at lunch counters. It is only to say governmentally required integration provided an opportunity to see new possibilities in human relations.

Returning to the distinction between government and morality, we can easily imagine just the opposite: government could have produced the opposite effect reinforcing segregation. Why didn't it? Was it the will of the people? Was it the will of the majority of the people? Perhaps it was merely the will of the government, the elected officials. Perhaps it was really the will of those who advise them, or, perhaps the will of the seemingly eternal governmental staff of the various federal bureaucracies. The separation of government and society from the standpoint of ethics may begin to look real.

To make this separation easier to see, consider the statement "Dropping the second atomic bomb on Japan was right." The statement has at least two meanings. First, "Most Americans were in favor of dropping the second atomic bomb." Second, "It was the right thing to do." I have used the second atomic bombing of Japan as my example to avoid some of the emotional reaction that may have been dominant at the time of the first bombing. There was deep concern about the loss of American lives if Japan would have to be invaded and the desire to obtain Japan's capitulation without it. The use of the atomic bomb seemed calculated to achieve just that. Also, World War II had been long fought and after a surprise attack by the Japanese on Pearl Harbor. So on August 9, 1945 the second atomic bomb was dropped on Nagasaki resulting in 39,000 killed outright and 25,000 injured with 40% of the city's buildings destroyed. But the second atomic bomb was dropped while the political and military effects of the first atomic bomb, that dropped on Hiroshima, were still being felt in Japan.

Without arguing for or against this action here and considering only what it means to say it was right, could we say it was right because it was the will of the American people? First, of all did the American people even know it was going to happen? No, they did not, but the proper reply is that their government had been elected to pursue the war for them and they expected that certain military actions in time of war would have to be planned and executed in secret. But the elected government was only that chosen to conduct the war by a majority of Americans. Lately we have had elections to office of a president by electoral votes and not even a majority of the voters. Presumably he could carry out a similar action. It is questionable just what the American people would have done had the dropping of the second bomb been put to a vote. Probably a majority would have voted for it. But they were not asked and legally did not have to be asked, and that is really all that needs to be said to show that governmental actions can be quite independent of the moral will of the society.

But suppose every governmental action did reflect the will of the majority of the people. Would that mean what the government does is morally right? It should be clear that the majority itself may be guided by momentary emotions, such as those prevalent at the time of World War II, resulting in regrettable actions. What most people think may or may not be morally correct. Only what furthers the purpose of the society is the determiner of right and wrong, and, as we have seen, what that is in itself is often difficult to determine and even more difficult to put into governmental action.

We are best reminded of what exactly majority rule means in government. It is a decision method, not a determiner of moral truth. Because our social aim is difficult to determine and our commands to our rulers often have to be given before there is moral consensus, we have agreed to let a majority of the members of the society decide. Equating morality with that means whatever the majority decides is morally right, and that cannot be true. We must always reserve the right to critique morally governmental action. But those who make government their source of morality are morally hamstrung. They think that if they can get government to do what they think is right, then they have determined what is right. Except for the fact that they have omitted moral considerations utterly, their reasoning is impeccable.

Despite majorities and elections, in modern times permanent governmental staffs employed by government but not elected to it have held great sway over the affairs of most societies. Anyone with experience in employee relations knows how difficult it is to discharge any employee, especially government employees. Employment protections of all sorts abound, from age, sex, and race discrimination to various forms of tenure rights. These, no doubt, are intended to serve the good purpose of employment security and protect personal and political freedom, and even insure continuity in governmental operations. For example, Richard Nixon's sensational presidential visit to China in 1972 was the result of Nixon's keen sense of international diplomacy, as well as the result of efforts by his formidable Secretary of State Henry Kissinger, but it was also the result of decades long effort by the United States Department of State.

Even so, the result of immense and virtually permanent governmental department staffs has been to create an imposing and parental presence upon the society of supposedly free adults. Gertrude Himmelfarb, professor emeritus of history at the Graduate School of the City University of New York and author of *The De-Moralization of Society*[4] tells that when she was writing that book, she wrote to a federal agency to inquire about the latest statistics on illegitimate births. She received a letter firmly rebuking her for using the term "illegitimate." She was told that the proper term is either "nontraditional childbearing" or "alternative modes of parenting."

To her this was legitimizing illegitimacy. Whether it was or not, it illustrates how government can have a will of its own. This is not the kind of thing that gets put to a vote. It is in most ways a minor point, but it does bear directly on morality. An inversion occurs: for uncritical thinkers the government, their moral guide, has spoken; for traditional thinkers, their government is illegitimizing their values. The reply to this has been an affirmation of pluralism. There are many values: traditional and nontraditional. In a free country, everyone is free. But without common purpose sought by common methods, there is no society.

Modern governments are also morally limited in another way. They are easily influenced by political action committees and other concentrations of money given to support candidates in their search of re-election in return for governmental decisions favoring the special interests of donors. Just as with overweening bureaucracies the cultivation and satisfaction of special interests separates the government and society. Unless the government is responsive to the will of the people, it is not an instrument of the people and has no moral basis. It becomes a separate entity. The same is true when the personnel of government become permanent without substantial rotation of new citizens into governmental operations and the role of ruling.

The separation of the rulers and the ruled becomes fixed, and there is a resulting loss of voluntary cooperation, an essential condition for a true society to exist. No human community is perfect in the sense of requiring no government. Every community will require a government because it is always becoming. But the government that helps to integrate those in the community who either do not know or voluntarily accept their social responsibilities will remain responsible to its people and not become a second layer society of absolute rulers crushing the free association essential to a moral community. Government, while necessary to a moral community, can never fully represent the moral sense of that community. Attempts by government perceived as doing so lead to anti-government movement. Indeed, such attempts can cause the loss of the moral force that makes the community a true society.

Finally, the relationship between government, the ruler, and society, the ruled, remains sound as long as the ruler willingly leads and the ruled willingly follow, but the ruler must also willingly follow the lead of the ruled. There is a mutuality in the relationship. Each must adapt to the other or else we have a situation where the ruler exercises raw power just because he has it, exerting his will over the others. And the ruled are allowing themselves to be dominated rather than led. Further, for free adults to give up consent to being ruled without becoming slaves and risking the loss of purpose, the ruler must be one who wills for them what they cannot will for and by themselves. That is the role of government. What government is to do cannot always be told in advance. General limits may be imposed by the governed, but the fact of living in history makes it impossible to anticipate everything the government may find itself called upon to do.

This explains why the character of the rulers, our leaders, is relevant among the claims society has upon them. That a society needs to be ruled at all means that every member of the society is not beyond being driven by personal desire, emotion, or other weakness in carrying out one's responsibilities for the common good. It is right to define a moral society as composed of free individuals, but they are free in the sense that they have voluntarily chosen to work and live together for the life benefits they can achieve together. They are not free in the sense of having perfect will to choose only that which is rational and best for themselves at all times. Each of us knows that there are times when we are in perfect control of ourselves and we can decide freely. But there are also times when the circumstances are such that we lose control as when carried away by our emotions.

This is equally true of groups of humans. The society can anticipate encountering stresses that could cause the society to break down. The society is not able to decide for itself what must be done. Historians have described Germany in the 1930's in just such a way.[5] Societies can lose the joint will that makes them societies. To protect the society against such a state of affairs, the members choose from among themselves leaders, individuals who show the strength of character to resist the vicissitudes of political events that may befall the society. That is why the leaders we choose must be individuals of integrity and personal strength. We count on them to do what most of us cannot, even to resist us when we are carried away by loss of will and in danger of losing our joint will and doing other foolish things.

The contemporary view of political leadership, the technological view, is a leader's character does not matter as long as he is capable of handling the affairs of state. This view makes sense only if one defines "capable" broadly enough to include having strength of character when necessary or "affairs of state" narrowly enough to exclude anything that will require strength of character. The distinction between a leader's private life and public life is a false one from the standpoint of assessing the person's ability to lead. What a person does in his private life can be very revealing about the strength of character required to hold a society together in times of stress. For example a married leader who commits adultery is a person who has given his word to a person, namely his spouse, that he will not commit adultery. If that same leader expects his followers to take his word and follow him in a course of action they are afraid to take themselves and they do, then they are themselves a collection of adulterers, a pack of fools, or both.

It is stylish to say a leader's private life does not matter. After all, Europeans allow their leaders personal freedom as long as they are discreet and do not embarrass their governments. Many Americans still believe what the Europeans do should be their guide, as if Europeans have always been blessed with leadership of distinction and integrity. Maybe it should, but the interpretation of European behavior in this regard is superficial. Europeans have the practice of handling the personal transgressions of their leaders in a discreet manner intended to avoid undermining confidence in their governments. The political leaders also do not make it a rule to pose as morally perfect in their marriages to get votes from those who believe in honorable marriages.

Of greater moral concern is the tolerance and voyeurism of the public who have come to expect and delight in the lurid private life details of their political candidates and leaders, something similar to what has been happening with the public and their media stars. This indicates we may be chosing our leaders in part from admiration for their "life styles," something we probably would like to emulate if we could, rather than their statesmanship. In other words we are chosing our leaders on the basis of character, and that character, or lack thereof, is what we admire. Our leaders are projecting our real values.

Another consideration lies in the familiar distinction between private and public life. Traditionally, a discrepency between how one behaves in public and how one behaves in private is hypocrisy. Lately we have come to assume our private life is our own business and our public life is something else altogether. Pluralism is the watchword. Each of us may do whatever we wish as long as it does not "interfere" with others doing the same. It is, then, the same with our leaders. We can have professing Roman Catholics publicly supporting federally funded abortions, even though they, presumably, do not believe in abortion themselves. The rationale is that we live in a pluralistic society. One who does not believe in abortion does not have to have one. The falsity of this distinction shows when government requires those who do not believe in them to pay for those who do.

This is not to open yet another discussion of abortion, but to show that one cannot in a moral community make a clean distinction between public and private morality. There are certain matters of our private life that do not affect the social purpose. But, by definition, these are not moral matters; they are personal ones. Indeed, it is only when our actions have a bearing on our common purpose that they are moral at all. Here one pauses because of the strong sense that morality is private. It is not.

Morality is often about private things such as sexual intercourse, the individual's decision to keep a promise, tell a lie, steal. But all of these less than public acts have a public bearing. A society can tolerate fornicators for a very long time before it is affected. It will tolerate fornicators until funding care for unwed mothers too young to work and care for the babies becomes unbearable. It will tolerate them until the mothers and fathers who do not know how to care for or support their babies become burdens on those who have had the will to be socially responsible for their own sexual behavior.

This same failure to see the social consequences of the belief that morality is "personal," has led to the idea that a leader's personal life is irrelevant to his fitness to lead. What the leader does in his private life has as much bearing on the social purpose as that of the rest of us. If we embrace an adulterous leader, we embrace adultery for ourselves. By the way, it is the same in the case of media stars, including professional athletes. In the past it was possible to tolerate the ways of the stars as an outlet for our own hidden desires. Now, the lives of our stars and leaders are practically the only moral example young people have. Why should they be exceptions to the moral expectations of society rather than paragons of morality?

In the case of leaders, however, they are supposed to be chosen precisely because they are paragons. They are chosen because they have strength where the rest of us have weakness. If they do not, then we do not need them to complicate things by holding power in the form of authority over us. If we cannot expect them to withstand the temptations we cannot or might not, then we are no better off with them than without them. Since we cannot know what every one of those temptations will be, we look for strength of character in our leaders. Also we assign certain privileges to our leaders, privileges to aid them in the difficult tasks we cannot do for ourselves. For example, we allow an official residence to our chief administrative officer. That makes it easier for him to do the job we want done for us. The idea is not that he deserves it by virtue of being our leader. The error we fall into in thinking this is assigning certain license to our leaders or their taking it, anyway, assuming it is part of their assigned powers as leaders.

The paragon of virtue role may seem too much to assign to political leaders. Yet that is integral to the relationship between ruler and ruled. The ruler is expected to spearhead the direction of the people, take them where they want to go but cannot by themselves. There is a mutuality as well. The ruled also shape how the ruler will rule. The ruler could try to extinguish the will of the people and make them follow him blindly. That would destroy utterly any semblance of society and make the people into slaves. The ruler has to get people to will with him the direction in which they want to go. Otherwise, he is merely floating on the waves of sentiment of an unruly mob. There must be a "shaped" direction. The leader of weak character cannot withstand the forces impacting on society and continues to appear to be a leader only by coincidence or good luck. Meanwhile, the society he is supposed to lead is without leadership and subject to all of the hazards that entails.

From these limitations of government and from these requirements of leadership, we can conclude that most modern nations are not moral communities. They are hopefully in process of becoming societies, or, better, they will always be composed of two parts—the society and the non-social community from which the society is seeking to form itself. This dynamic relationship between these two parts is such that there is always the possibility that the social part will break down and dissolve into the non-societal part, something hardly distinguishable from a mob. The standing error in contemporary political thought is believing nations are complete societies and all of the so called conflicts over values can be resolved by greater tolerance and the encouragement of pluralism.

This error leads to the lawlessness and immorality we are experiencing because the internal logical inconsistency in it means anything goes. Any semblance of morality results from the existence of numerous pocket societies, groups of people living responsibly toward one another and more or less at peace. They may become involved in a central economy allowed to operate without moral control. Hence, it should be no surprise that industrial pollution and other forms of dishonesty abound. As long as those in charge of them believe they and their families are not affected at home in their moral pocket, they conclude there is no harm done.

Considering how long something similar existed during the middle ages, there is no reason to believe mixture of morality, immorality, and amorality cannot continue for a long time. But it does not have to be like this, and if we think the crime and immorality we see all around us are intolerable, we can do something about it. Moreover, even if things are not intolerable, despite all of the lip service to the contrary, we are missing an opportunity for greatness by perpetuating this subversion of morality by government. There are permanent, underlying values in the nations. The people, and especially their leaders, only have to look for them and press them forward.

Several years ago in the United States the National Endowment for the Humanities undertook to discover the ideals that Americans held in common. Extensive interviews including some with new Vietnamese immigrants who could hardly speak English revealed two that pervade the American political tradition: freedom and equality. Those interviewed were aware of some of the best American laws, the Declaration of Independence, the Constitution and the Bill of Rights, but the ideals of freedom and equality were uppermost in their minds. This was because they experienced a strong sense of freedom and equality living in the United States.

Freedom and equality are concepts found in our time most commonly in political contexts. But it does not follow from this that they are the gifts of government. They are the ideational products of the human ascent toward civilization, the teachings of philosophers and prophets, and even the struggle against governments. Before they are expressed in government documents they are the property of the society forming or reacting to the government. Consider the many governments stating the ideals of freedom and equality whose people in reality have nothing of the kind. Freedom and equality come first to a people who will them into practice and design governments to help secure them.

Freedom and equality, no matter how widely shared by Americans, do not a national identity make, nor an ethical community. There are too many racial, ethnic, religious, and just plain unwashed communities within the national borders to expect general agreement on a common purpose or shared set of goals. This, by the way, is evidence the United States is not a society in the sense of being a moral community. The extent of lawlessness in the country gives witness to this. But even if freedom and equality are not sufficient to provide a complete morality, they do provide a beginning. To see how that might work, we must next examine what the vast ethnic diversity means for a community of people seeking to be a society.

Notes

1. Thomas Moore, *The Care of the Soul*, New York, Harper Collins, 1992, Chapter 10, p. 206.
2. *The Wall Street Journal*, November 6, 1996, p. A5.
3. *Ibid*
4. Gertrude Himmelfarb, *The De-Moralization of Society: From Victorian Virtues to Modern Values*, New York, A.A.Knopf, 1995.
5. William Lawrence Shirer, *The Rise and Fall of the Third Reich: A History of Nazi Germany*, New York, Simon and Shuster, 1960, pp. 150-87.

Chapter VII

ℰᎧᏻᏳ

Ethics, Ethnicity, and Diversity: The Members of the Crew

"Where have you gone Joe DiMaggio?
The nation turns its lonely eyes to you."
—Simon and Garfunkel, "Mrs.Robinson"

The center of a society is its moral bond, what the people believe they are about together. Without this among at least the adult members of the group there is no society, only humans collected on some basis, usually mere geography. Government is not this moral bond but, rather, rests upon it, even though it is common error to believe just the opposite. Governments come and go, but societies endure until they can form another government. A government cannot long endure after its sponsoring society crumbles. An examination of the growing diversity in the United States can help test the validity of the relationships between society and government and between a mere collection of people and a morally bound people, a society.

If there is a national identity in America, and there are reasons to believe there still is, it is being severely tested and in danger of being lost. Many social institutions have come dangerously close to disaster, and many American writers claim some of them are already dysfunctional because they are creatures of a white European Christian tradition oppressive to minorities and women. In addition, certain minorities and women have wanted to assert their own traditions as more worthy of themselves and even more worthy of others as well. This has had its matching white and male counterparts.

The Nation of Islam's Khalid Abdul and followers, the American Neo-Nazis and the White Aryan Resistance have emerged on the national scene. There are the ethnic separatists such as Leonard Jeffries who reject the notion of American national identity and glorify African identity. There are the women's movement and the men's movement, and those who claim women are better than men and those who claim men are better than women, whatever either group may mean by that. There are militiamen who consider government, in its many forms in America, the enemy they must defeat. There is also the cultivation of political correctness with its host of sacred icons, and the cultivation of sexual orientation as if this were a matter of personal "life style."

Another tension point in the national identity arises when resident aliens and even American citizens try to influence United States foreign politics for the benefit of another nation rather than the United States. Also, overweening concern for illegal aliens by resident aliens and even citizens is having a divisive effect on the maintenance of a national identity. Readers can add to this seemingly unending list.

One of the most disturbing threats is to the judicial system. This has become a matter of sharp focus since the Rodney King and the O.J. Simpson cases. Polls taken at the time of the Simpson trial indicated that 60% of whites polled believed Simpson would receive a fair trial, and only 30% of blacks polled believed he would. Just a few years earlier, the courts were seen as the real hope for achieving racial equality in America. Justice was supposed to be color blind.

Such reflections have led both conservative Linda Chavez[1] and liberal Arthur Schlesinger[2] to urge a return to America as "melting pot," a place where people of different national, racial, and ethnic backgrounds would grow into one national identity, one society. The people of this society would remember their different heritage, but they would still be one people. The differences in background would be minor in comparison to the new American nationality. But how, exactly, is this supposed to work? What part of the old nationalities is supposed to recede and what continue, and what makes the new nationality?

What usually comes to mind to moderns is a geopolitical identity, being under the jurisdiction of an independent or sovereign national government. For some of the people of the United States this is defined historically, too. The Revolutionary War and the Civil War were complex events but nevertheless definitive of our nationality. Other wars and other major events affecting the general population had their triumphs and defeats, their heroes and villains. For others the United States is defined economically. It is the land of opportunity where one can become wealthy and the sky is the limit. These, too, have their heroes in the person of tycoons. For others the definition is cultural, based on the European heritage, and the Judeo-Christian tradition. These, too, have their saints and sinners, their writers, artists, and prophets.

Recently, others have emerged defining America as the land of the free, free for all, not limited by tradition or history but only by our individual ability to create new things and new relationships, a place where there are no boundaries and where national identity is a little naive.[3] There are no limits to what an individual can be. Fulfillment of one's desires as that individual understands them is purpose enough. These, too, have their heroes and villains. They are filmmakers, film and television stars, international celebrities, and sports figures. Photographic and cinema graphic images stimulate fantasies to fascinate and to pursue, desires to fulfill and things to buy or otherwise obtain. There are many more such configurations, and each has its family, friends, and social and business connections presenting additional bonds and requiring its own rituals and rules of behavior.

These groups do not stand independently of one another. They are interrelated as well. Some of the churches in America, for example, have supported illegal immigrants in acts joining them with the nontraditionalists who see no national boundaries. Newscasters and public television thinkers make claims suggesting a whole from this patchwork. These are their observations and opinions on an extremely complex phenomenon. Who does not recall hearing a Briton or European giving a "you Americans" talk? Others use statistics about what Americans buy or how they vote or how often their marriages end in divorce. In this way they describe what looks like a national identity running through the religious, ethnic, racial, and national origin differences of those who populate the United States.[4]

That, however, does not make a society. What does is what the people themselves think unites them, not how they can be described by an "outside" observer, but what they themselves intend to be together as a people. If my buying patterns or any other behavior patterns are the same as those of the person living in the same apartment building as I do, we are not necessarily bound in any relationship at all, and neither of us may even know the other exists, let alone care. His life matters not in the least to me nor mine to him. To be joined in any meaningful relationship each of us must first acknowledge it, and, even more, we must intend to be related. Each of us must know what we are about together, and we must will that we continue to be, and each of us must see this as part of our lives.

"No man is an island," as the poet John Donne writes. But unless a person sees how he relates to others, he can only concur with Shakespeare's Macbeth who, alienated from his life and relationships by his traitorous acts, utters:

Life's but a walking shadow, a poor player
That struts and frets his hour upon the stage
And then is heard no more: it is a tale
Told by an idiot, full of sound and fury,
Signifying nothing.

If we bother to think about the meaning of our life, we are reluctant to conclude it signifies nothing. To believe life signifies something, though, requires seeing one's life as a story and not a series of disconnected events. How does this happen?

An individual's story is made from relationships to others—family, friends, society at large. What happens to him and what he makes happen he interprets as part of some larger purpose. In most cases this is the life and activities of some group. One's identity comes from being the son or daughter of someone, baptized, circumcised, confirmed, married, employed, an Eskimo, Greek, Christian, Jew, African American, Mexican American, Japanese, Italian, Spanish, one or more of these and many others. But what is the source of the group identity? It is what they do, the way they do it, their conventions, beliefs, and history together, all coming as consciousness of what the group is.

These unique group histories and the moral practices they have created lead some thinkers to conclude morality is what the group believes it is, and all groups may not believe alike. Because there are so many different moral practices among the different cultures what is right is determined by what the group believes. The consequences for a pluralistic country like the United States are staggering. If different cultures have different standards of moral conduct, then the multicultural United States cannot begin to be a society of individuals bound together voluntarily by common purpose into a moral community. At best, it is a collection of peoples loosely affiliated by state and local law, and if common assent is the foundation of law, the extensive lawlessness in the United States today should be no surprise.

Whatever the basis of difference and diversity, the issue is, Can a moral unity emerge from them? Can the people of "Queer Nation" live in harmony with the Christian fundamentalists who consider the practice of homosexuality an invitation to fire and brimstone? For its myriad of ramifications, the moral dilemma caused by the growing radical diversity in America looks very much like the classical ethical problem posed by cultural relativism.

In the United States we are especially inept at dealing with this kind of problem because of the current excess of sentiment among intellectuals and journalists that all beliefs are equal. No doubt, much of this is a reaction to the centuries of European and American colonial domination of many other countries and cultures. It may also be reaction to economic and military dominance of the United States and the ever present ugly American tourist throughout the world. These speculations need to be tempered in light of the contemporary global mood of some who take heart in seeing American franchises, tee shirts and blue jeans, and popular music seeming to signify protest against national traditions spread throughout the world by means of mass media.

Even so, a certain mawkishness still obtains when these people look at other cultures, especially those we used to call primitive. Also, when considering Central and South American countries, there is an irrepressible fondness for revolutionaries whatever their moral character. All things considered, all peoples and all of their beliefs are equal. This is cultural relativism. No one culture is mistaken in its beliefs especially about what to do and not to do. What is right or wrong is a matter of how one was raised and what the people around the person do.

To gain some perspective on the problem, compare two cultures remote from each other—the Eskimo and the American Midwesterners.[5] The Eskimo have lived in relative isolation but on the northern edge of North America. While it may be difficult to argue that the American Midwest has its own culture, I shall for purposes of discussion hold out small town Minnesotans and Iowans as making an American subculture of traditionally conservative moral beliefs. It is hard to find typical conservative values in North America, but if they exist anywhere it is among these people. Eskimo culture has changed through growing contact with Europeans and North Americans, and it is difficult to learn exactly what their beliefs and customs really are and the real reasons they act the way they do. Even so, we have reports from early explorers relating Eskimo customs that shock and even horrify American Midwesterners.

Consider Eskimo customs regarding sex and procreation. Not only did many of the men have more than one wife, but shared their wives with guests, even letting wives and guests sleep together overnight as a form of hospitality. While some raucous parties even in the Midwest might end up that way, it would not likely be planned as a courtesy and more likely characterized the next day as the result of too much alcohol and otherwise wild enthusiasm. Also, among the Eskimo, prominent males can expect sexual relations with other men's wives. Such favors in America are granted, too, among intellectuals for visiting poets and novelists and among modern mass culture people for athletes, rock and film stars, and other leading media personalities. But it could hardly be said to be the custom among small town Iowans. Eskimo women also had the freedom to leave their husbands and go off with a new male as long as the previous male chose not to interfere. While this is much like the living together arrangements common in the American Midwest, it contrasts sharply with the idea of marriage as defined by the major religions and laws in the United States.

It is in matters of life and death that the Eskimo contrasts most with the American Midwesterner and, indeed, most people in the United States. It is in this contrast we learn most about relativism and about the problems of life and death facing us in the United States today. One famous explorer, Knud Rasmussen, reported that one Eskimo woman he met had given birth to twenty children.[6] She, herself, had killed ten of them at birth. This was not uncommon among the Eskimo. Female babies were most likely to be killed, but male babies were killed, too. The decision to kill the baby was entirely for the parents alone; there were no societal rules against it. This is shocking even today. We are accustomed to the widespread use of abortion, and we are aware of the practice of partial birth abortions, but killing a baby after it is born must appear even to the most radical advocates of choice among us the worst of moral offenses.

Refusing to assist the elderly incapable of fending for themselves and even killing them was also not uncommon among the Eskimo. By some accounts a son would kill his parents when they became incapable of providing for themselves. In contrast, in ancient Rome and practically all nations influenced by Roman law, the killing of a father by a son is regarded a heinous offense.

Sharing wives, killing babies and killing parents are so contary to our moral thinking that our initial reaction is to consider the Eskimo primitive, barbaric people with no sense of right and wrong. But, on second thought, those of us who have grown more sophisticated on these matters, those of us who have moved from small town Iowa to Los Angeles, say, we know it is naive to expect everyone to follow the same practices. There are, after all, "alternative life styles," "open marriages," "free love" aficionados, those who are "for choice" in dealing with pregnancy, even Dr. Kervorkian and his followers who advocate terminating one's own life when it is not of the "quality" one desires. Now there are those who advocate letting others die or even euthanizing them when it becomes too expensive or too tedious to support their lives.

It appears we can only hasten to conclude that our ideas of right and wrong are just not going to be held by everyone, especially those of different cultures. Hence, there are no absolutes in ethics. There are only those customs which a culture has, and not all cultures have the same ones. Indeed, they have conflicting ones. "Ethics is relative to the culture." This is the doctrine of ethical relativism. According to this doctrine, the Eskimo are not barbaric; they are just different. Similarly the moral practices in the subcultures of the United States are neither right nor wrong; they are what they are. On this doctrine we can now happily go on being "open minded" and sophisticated tolerating whatever people choose to do because "its all right for them." Anyone trying to argue them into doing differently is a narrow minded naive absolutist and probably a religious fundamentalist.

To avoid confusion on a key point it is necessary to interject that there is a difference between ethical relativism and barbarism. It is one thing to say that each culture has its own ethical code. It is quite another to say that because practices regarding procreation and protection of life in one culture are different from the practices in one's own culture they are not moral at all. For example, polygamy is different from monogamy, but there are ways to do each of them morally and there are ways to do each of them immorally. A polygamist could conceivably be unfaithful to his wives and adulterous by having sexual relations with the wife of another or with an unmarried woman. In a polygamous culture this would be immoral, even though it is moral to have more than one wife. In a monogamous culture one could be unfaithful to his wife by having sexual relations with another woman or having more than one wife.

The ethical relativist says because different cultures have different moral codes there is no objective way to condone or condemn the moral codes of different cultures. One's own moral code is but one among many. It seems that what we do is right just because we are used to it. We protect our babies in the Midwest, and the Eskimos don't in the Arctic. It is merely ethnocentric to say our way is right and their way is not.

But does it follow that what is right and wrong is only relative? Does it follow from the fact that Eskimos and Midwesterners would disagree about infanticide, there is no ethically objective way to settle the disagreement? Even at home we seem to think so: some of us say we don't believe in divorce, but we understand that our friends down the street do. We would not think of calling them immoral because they have a different set of beliefs or a "different life style." This is the way many young people treat one another on moral matters. They accept these ethical ambiguities and look on those who try to reject them as old fashioned judgmental moralists who are not with it. "As long as it doesn't hurt anyone, its all right."

The flaw in this reasoning is viewing individual action too narrowly. In the harsh environment of the Eskimo with its scarcity of food and overall struggle for survival, the responsible individual found it necessary to end the lives of the elderly who could not care for themselves in order to be able to care for themselves and their young. Taking the lives of the elderly to save the lives of the young and to save the elderly from lingering death because of lack of nutrition is the moral thing to do in contrast to trying not to hurt anyone and as a consequence risking all lives. Similarly infanticide might be required to avoid overpopulation and starvation. No doubt, the Eskimo believed females were less valuable in that regard because they were not food producers in their hunter culture and the males were.

Faced with these harsh choices we might all come to moral practices similar to those of the Eskimo. As techniques for prolonging life in our society improve and their costs continue to mount, euthanasia for the elderly will become a more attractive option even to us. Already ethicists are asking if we are not spending too much of our resources on keeping people alive with "poor quality of life."[7] The central force of the argument is directed against spending research and treatment dollars to keep elderly alive through expensive organ transplants and other procedures instead of finding treatments for illnesses afflicting the young who have enjoyed only short lives and could, if well, contribute to society in ways the elderly no longer can.

There is much more to be said on this issue, and arguments to be made on behalf of the elderly. After all, the elderly have made their contribution and perhaps ought to be entitled to the security benefit of knowing they will receive care when they cannot care for themselves. But the point here is not to argue that. It is rather that when faced with life and death decisions of this sort, people, whatever their cultures, tend to react in similar ways. They tend to do what they think is a life maximizing act. This means that the cultural differences the ethical relativists are so fond of emphasizing, when examined beneath the surface, are not really ethical differences at all. There are great similarities in ethical behavior when the nature and meaning of the actions are fully understood in the context of the environmental challenges and the extent of the peoples' knowledge.

As knowledge and information increase among cultures and physical limitations are removed, people of different cultures tend to act in similar ways. When Eskimo find they do not have to reduce the number of infants and elderly for the population to survive, they tend to stop doing it. The common purpose of peoples is the same: security and survival through cooperation. The Eskimo who could not take responsibility in controlling family infants and elderly would be considered weak and immoral because he risks insupportable overpopulation, making poor use of scarce resources needed for the survival of those who can do the most for the lives of everyone else.

Now it is possible that a people lock themselves into moral duties of this sort based on poor understanding of their situation. They may think they must conduct themselves in certain ways when they in fact do not. A useful example is the blood feud, a state of conflict between two groups, usually kinship groups, within a society. The blood feud involves violence in the form of killings and revenge killings. Those who conduct blood feuds believe their honor calls for revenge in the form of killing one of the kin of those who killed their kin; or payment of some other form of compensation, sometimes payment known as blood money. One kinship group holds another responsible for an injury to its member suffered at the hands of a member of another kinship group. These people could easily avoid bloodshed by creating a judicial system to promote harmony beyond the feud system and make life better for all concerned. But they don't know that or are not about to abdicate their sense of honor. We understand this from cowboy movies, football teams rivalries, and the Hatfields and the McCoys.

This does not mean the feud system is right and the judicial system is right, too. When it operates properly, the judicial system is better. So that they continue to feud does not mean there is no right or wrong. It only means that they do not know any better, and it is an egregious error for us as ethical thinkers to believe that right and wrong are merely in the folkways of diverse cultures. What people believe is one thing; what is right is another. Folkways are custom, habit, and ritual. Ethics are principles, the product of reason and reflection. A tribesman does not ask whether the custom is right or wrong for he has no way to assess it. An ethical person does ask whether his actions are right or wrong and even whether the principles according to which he acts are right or wrong.

The gap between doing what one has always done and doing what one believes after moral reflection is enormous. Much has happened for mankind to go from the former to the latter and not all peoples have. That people behave differently in different cultures does not prove they ought to act differently; only that they do. The ethicist must still ask whether what they are doing is right or wrong. Modern squeamishness about doing so has many roots, and some of them have been mentioned earlier. But confusion about the difference between cultural relativism and ethical relativism has been the culprit among intellectuals. Their sense of fairness and open-mindedness in the spirit of "Who are we to judge others?" has caused great confusion.

Nietzsche may have sat empty at the philosophers' table, but philosophers have unraveled this and other major confusions about culture and ethical relativism, and their clarity of thought should be recognized. Too long have the moralists, ministers, lawyers, psychologists, sociologists, and anthropologists sat in splendid isolation at their own tables pondering and pronouncing on substantial moral questions without the benefit of the rational analyses prepared for them by the philosophers. Let's look at some of them.

First, what originally appears to us to be radical differences in values from one culture to another ends up not being so radical once we consider the differences in beliefs and living conditions of the cultures. It is not because the Eskimo do not value life they kill infants; they believe they have to kill infants to protect life. They tend to kill female babies rather than male babies, but the mortality of males in that hunter culture is much higher than females. If the people are to survive, they must have as many hunters as possible. It cannot be they want to kill babies because no people failing to protect and nurture their young could endure. They feel forced to kill so some might survive in their harsh and insecure environment. Faced with that agonizing choice, most people would probably do the same. Fortunately, most of us will not have to face such a choice. Some of us, from our fortunate circumstances, may say that killing any infant, no matter what the circumstances, is absolutely wrong. But what if really faced with the choice of killing one of your children so that three of them could live? What happens to your absolute, then?

Second, we can see other points where we might not be so far different morally from Eskimo when we consider all of the facts and circumstances of these humans as they make the choices we call moral. In the Midwest people put a premium on trust. You have to be able to trust people. Otherwise there would be no credit, information people gave us would be unreliable, and we could depend on no one. Eskimo may not have had a banking system, but they had to rely on one another to keep their word and to tell the truth. Imagine an arctic hunter lost in a snowstorm chancing upon another whom he asks for directions to the nearest shelter. There is no room for anything but the most reliable honest answer. Could any people survive in such circumstances with anything less? That, as I explained in Chapter III, goes to the essence of morality: mutual reliance for survival.

That is why no society permits its members indiscriminate killing of one another. There may be rare exceptions believed to be necessity such as population control through infanticide, or capital punishment. But no one is secure and no society can endure long enough for mutual reliance unless it controls very strictly how and when the life of a member is taken. Clearly, a society that allows a member to take the life of another member for a pair of shoes or a leather jacket cannot expect to achieve much or even continue.

Third, this leads to another lesson moral philosophers have taught us: not all moral rules are culture dependent and some similar moral rules will be found in every society because they are essential for the existence of any society. Because we are mortal beings and we live in a changing world with hazards to life on every side we must choose to act in certain very similar ways or we place ourselves at very serious risk.

Fourth, what in our own culture we consider absolute because it is habitual, seems natural or intuitive, may not be absolute at all. As long as conditions remain the same, we can cling to certain general rules. But, as soon as they change, we become restless and make exceptions. "Thou shalt not kill," unless there is too much killing and then we try killing the killers to reduce the killing, unless there is too much medical technology and we don't know how to care for so many people on life support systems, unless there is too much sustained abuse for a spouse to endure. There are going to be general patterns of moral behavior found in every society and there are going to be exceptions. The exceptions will vary from society to society because of the specific conditions experienced in each.

But a society makes exceptions to these universal patterns at its very great peril. If you are going to make an exception to the rule against killing, you had better be sure of what you are doing. The pattern is there in the first place for a very good reason. This is what has given us the idea that there are moral absolutes. It is the stuff of which pacifists and religious absolutists are born. It is so very wrong to kill that it is easy to say we should never kill a human being under any circumstances. It is so very wrong to lie that we should never tell a lie. That way one's conscience is always clear. But who will protect life when it needs protecting? There is a belief in a form of providence in these minds. What warrants the belief? What do we do until the force begins to take hold? Never tell a lie? Suppose an enemy intent on murdering your child demands to know where the child is? "Well, in that case. . . ." How does this case differ from lying to a fellow citizen asking for directions you are embarrassed to admit you don't know?

In this and in all cases where exceptions to the rule are made you must ask why we have the rule in the first place. That will tell you when exceptions are appropriate. You kill someone intent on killing you when there is no other way to stop the person because staying alive is what the rule against killing is about. You lie to an enemy intent on killing your child because telling the truth is not about that but, rather, about working honestly with people you trust who are working with you. You follow these rules when you share a common purpose, when you are working together in a relationship of trust and cooperation. How we determine who this is from time to time and place to place is often problematic. In the next chapter we consider to whom we are morally responsible.

Fifth, just as there are similar moral rules found in every society, there are other moral rules that are not. Historically, in Europe, Africa, and India it has been customary for the wife or her family to give the husband a dowry at the time of the marriage. This custom is not practiced and even little known in the American Midwest. In places where the dowry is given it is a substantial gift and often burdensome for the wife or her family to give. The average Midwesterner would consider it an unfair custom whereby males exact a price for the marriage. But in some societies the dowry has served to protect the wife from the husband because it was a conditional gift. If the husband divorced the wife or offended her in some way, he would have to give it back. Also, if the husband died or became incapacitated, the wife would take the dowry for her own security regardless of what happened to the husband's property. Other aspects of this practice still survive even in American law known as dower rights.

The point is not so much to justify the practice as to show it is difficult to say whether it is either right or wrong merely by comparison to the way marriage customs work in the Midwest. There are different ways to go about marriage and provide for the bride and groom. In certain places a marriage without a dowry is looked down upon as tasteless. To a Midwesterner it would be hard to understand the fuss. But the ethical relativist wants to argue that because these customs are culture dependent moral practices are, too, and so there is nothing objective in judgments of right and wrong. We have been able to see the error in this reasoning.

Sixth, in looking across cultures we can learn that we should not be quick to judge the ways of other people. Looking beyond the surface appearance of their acts and examining the full context wherein they act, we can see that much of what they are trying to do flows from values very similar to ours. Given that we are all what we are, we really shouldn't expect anything else. Also, even if there are some cultural differences such as giving of dowries, they do not really clash with ours; they are only different.

Now let's go back to those in culturally diverse America who want to go their separate ways because of ethnic, religious, or ethical differences. What, exactly, are they saying? Are they ethical relativists saying that they have their ways and they are different from the ways of other subcultures in America and, therefore, do not want to be held to alien standards of behavior? Then we have to examine these differences to see if, indeed, they represent genuine moral disagreement or merely the kind of superficial differences we can expect across cultures. Are they ethical absolutists, saying their ways are the only correct ways? Then they have to show that, in light of all we have seen here about comparing cultures, they have the only true way and the ways of others are mistaken.

Are they saying these are just differences, in which case we can ask, then, do they matter enough to cause divisions among us and make moral community among us impossible? We can discuss these differences and weigh their significance against the practically universal common human purposes of survival, security, social stability, and self-realization. Do we differ about child rearing, marriage, sexuality, cooperation, trust, honesty, diligence, reliability? If we do differ, it is possible that we are not sharing the same facts in which case we can come to the table to share information. If cultures all over the world tend to converge on moral practices when they possess the same facts, then it is likely American subcultures will.

Now it is quite possible that some or all of these people advocating separation or radical social change based on their own beliefs are not relativists but absolutists. They are right and everyone else is wrong. That position would be hopelessly fractious for the people of the United States. But as the philosophers have taught us about ethical diversity, we do not have to let the matter end there. Probably in Pago Pago the people do think their prescribed conduct is just right and as it ought to be. As we have already seen, though, mere ethnic practice will not suffice as moral justification. We were not morally content to allow slavery in parts of the United States on the ground that it is a part of the Southern subculture. We are hardly content to conscience torture of animals or people in other countries, or to look with equanimity upon female circumcision in Nigeria or genocide in Germany, Russia, or Cambodia.

Mere ethnicity or subgroup practices are at the level of folkways, "in-group" behavior. They are not at the level of critical self-reflection on common purpose. They are narrowly focused without regard to the full implications of their behavior and how they affect others with whom they interact in daily existence. It is just here, where the habitual behavior of some conflicts with that of others, that moral reflection begins. That is the situation we are facing in America today. Everyone is right, somehow. As long as no conflicts arise, then everyone should go about his business as in the past. The hidden danger is that conflicts often do not arise immediately but after long term ethnic practices and so are not obvious in our usual short term legal and political analyses. Often we conclude there is no harm in certain behavior when there is but we cannot see it in the short run.

Consider the subjugation of individuals in a society in a semi-permanent underclass. A society can go for a considerable time treating the members of the underclass as less than equal to members of the ruling class, but social instability and its harmful consequences will eventually emerge. It may be economically advantageous and have utilitarian value to use some people even as slaves, but the immorality of the practice will eventually become apparent and then intolerable. Even a minority that uses the majority for its own benefit without voluntarily sharing goals with them will eventually be resented and treated as morally reprehensible. Thus, emphasizing ethnic diversity may have certain value, but not moral value. It is through ethics, not ethnicity, that people in modern societies discover how to share a common life for their betterment.

Ethnicity may even provide ethical value, but it may also provide ethical limitation. Certain ways of a people may be good for them, but they may also be bad. Consider for the moment an example from the economic sector rather than from the moral. In Southeast Asia overseas Chinese were not allowed to hold certain jobs. These Chinese had to pay extra taxes and to live in special areas, and they were even subjected to physical violence. Despite this, they were able to prosper beyond the poverty-stricken natives who tormented them. We must, of course, assume that the natives did not choose to live in poverty, but considering how they tormented their Chinese immigrants, it is not difficult to conclude that they resented the Chinese because they had what they themselves would have liked. From the standpoint of economic gain, then, the natives would have done better to adopt some of the work habits of the Chinese in place of their own. Resting content with their folkways, they remained poor while the Chinese became rich.[8]

It is similar with what people commonly call "morals." Among certain people it is or has become habitual to have children out of wedlock. They might even be amused at the sight of other people putting so much emphasis on quaint notions such as virginity and on marital fidelity because of the sexual frustration they cause and even the "hypocrisy" surrounding them. This contrast in attitudes toward sexuality and reproduction might exist between one culture and another, between one national subculture and another, or between one social class and another in the same culture. When we look at the personal and eventual social cost of the practices we can make an ethical evaluation and determine if either of the opposing moral practices is right. Possibly neither is ethically right: there may be a third and better way.

But neither is right just because one group of people or another says it is. Here we come upon the ultimate test of what makes a practice right: of all the ways we could go about this business, is this the best we can do for ourselves? In other words, is this what we must require of each of us in order to bring about the best situation for ourselves as a group and for each of us as an individual? Is this what we must require of each of us to bring about the best situation for all of us?

This is where most people fall off the wagon and into utilitarianism morass. They ask, does this way of doing things make for the greatest happiness for the greatest number? But happiness is only one possible common purpose. The common purpose is whatever a group thinks its best option is for its individuals consistent with the groups best information and techniques for attaining it. A common error is thinking this can be determined once and for all. We can, as humans, commit ourselves to looking for it, and we can even hold that most humans will begin to converge toward it once they have the same knowledge. But this is a complex matter of knowledge, freedom from ignorance and superstition.

Consider the practice of homosexuality. For those who advocate it, is it a folkway, a mere custom of a culture or subculture? If it is, it is appropriate to ask if it is right or wrong. Is it consistent with what we must require of one another to attain the common good? If after careful examination we find it is, then it can hardly be held to be wrong. But if it is inconsistent, does it interfere with what we are trying to accomplish with regard to procreation, interfere with marriage or the need for reproduction? Currently, in the Western world the practice of homosexuality tends to be viewed as a matter of individual rights. "Its my own business and I ought to be free to do what I want," "consenting adults," and the like. That is a possible approach to the practice, but it is very superficial and hardly raised to an ethical level.

The ethical question is whether the practice of homosexuality interferes with the rest of what we are trying to accomplish in regulating sexuality, its procreative aspects and the entailed relationships of trust. All of us are regulated in one way or another for the common purpose. Married males are expected to live monogamously, even though we know it is quite difficult for most of them. Children have been expected to abstain from sex until attaining some acceptable age. It may be the practice of homosexuality contributes to the common purpose. Since it basically does not result in childbirth, it might be helpful in an age of over fertility and, as some might argue, overpopulation. It may well be desirable to have aunts and uncles, who because they have no children of their own, can help parents raise children. But all of this has to be answered according to our best lights. It simply will not do to argue for homosexuality because it is "natural" or because it is no one's business what consenting adults do. Consenting adults do a lot of things that cannot be tolerated because they interfere with what we have to require of one another to meet our common purpose.

This brings us to those who want no part of the common purpose that interferes with their way of doing things. Some separatists would claim they are not even allowed to share the purpose and, consequently, have no duty to others, for example, minorities who believe they cannot get ahead because they are ruled by others and are not allowed to rule themselves. But that is really an empirical question. Are they benefiting from the society because everyone else is working for the common purpose, playing by the rules, so to speak? If they choose to separate, does that include giving up all such benefits, such as those of the economic system? Are the "moral" differences so significant it is worth giving up these benefits, or are there more really fundamental moral principles in common than for reasons of political power, or something else they are willing to admit? And, finally, do the beliefs impelling you in another direction really give you the possibilities for security and self-realization you seek?

Sometimes what appears as moral disagreement is mere lack of sensitivity to our real shared moral beliefs. After consideration, slavery, anti-Semitism, and the subjugation of women were rejected as morally reprehensible. We did not "see" we were being unfair in these practices even according to our own shared goals for security and self-realization. We were making unjustifiable exceptions in the way we treated certain people. It is helpful to recall that Martin Luther King, Jr. centered his efforts toward equality upon everyone's own sense of fairness by asking us to live according to our own moral beliefs.

And this brings us to the idea of moral responsibility. To whom are we responsible morally and who is responsible to us morally? Failure to seek meaningful answers to these two questions has brought us to the desperate level of morality today. We have quietly decided we will be responsible only to ourselves and to those we care about, leaving aside any questions about any others with whom we may have common purpose and who have common purpose with us. This is the subject of the next chapter.

Can a fractious society such as ours come together? Why could it not? We have seen fractious families come together in times of crisis, families where members seemed hopelessly alienated from one another. We have seen new life breathed into corporations or even into federal, state, and local governments. Why not consider breathing life into the nation? This is done in corporations by developing a mission and focusing everyone in the corporation upon the mission. Then each person takes a meaningful role in pursuing the mission with a specific assignment of responsibilities and rewards. Personnel not ready for the work are trained.

The comparisons to reuniting a society should be obvious, as should the shortcomings in moral vision of our society's leaders and the moral training we provide our members. None of it is impossible. It is not as though we have no idea what we must do. We are just not doing it. Having left the ethics of our society to lawyers, political parties, sectarian ministers, ethnic and racial leaders, and bureaucracies, we should not be surprised. It is time for those with common sense and the ability to think to step forward and lead. The central purpose of this book is to present a unified view of moral realities to help point the way.

Notes

1. Linda Chavez, *Out of the Barrio: Toward a New Politics of Hispanic Assimilation,* New York, Basic Books, 1991.
2. Arthur L. Schlesinger, *The Disuniting of America: Reflections on a Multicultural Society,* New York, W. W. Norton & Company, 1992.
3. A notion roundly criticized by Thomas Sowell, *The Vision of the Anointed,* New York, Basic Books, pp. 199-203.
4. For more on this, see Rupert Wilkinson, *The Pursuit of the American Character*, New York, Harper & Row, 1988.
5. This discussion relies on the excellent chapter entitled "The Challenge of Cultural Relativism" in *The Elements of Moral Philosophy* by James Rachels. Copyright © 1986 by Random House, Inc.
6. Knud Rasmussen, *Greenland by the Polar Sea*, New York, AMS Press, 1988.
7. See, for example, Daniel Callahan: "Aging and the Ends of Medicine". *Annals of the New York Academy of* Sciences, 530 (June 15, 1988), pp. 125-132.
8. Thomas Sowell, *Migrations and Cultures*, New York, Basic Books, 1996, Chapter 5.

Chapter VIII

ॐ

Moral Responsibility: Keeping the Watch

Then the Lord said to Cain, "Where is your brother Abel?"
"I don't know," he replied. "Am I my brother's keeper?"
—Genesis 4:9

Much has been written over the ages about moral responsibility, and yet the most commonly heard lament about morality in our age is over the lack of responsibility. An answer to whether or not we are our brother's and sister's keepers would go far in resolving the ethical dilemmas we are so quick to spin. As our sense of responsibility to one another shrinks, our moral confusion mounts. Do we owe anything to our family, our friends, our nation, other nations, people in our nation with different "life styles"and values? We withdraw into ourselves to find a secure place where we might reckon who are those we owe and who owe us. Most days we think we are safe concluding we owe only ourselves. But if we owe no one anything and no one owes us anything, then there is no such thing as morality.

What are we talking about when we talk of responsibility? There are five major dictionary senses of the word "responsible." Listing them gives a feel for the subject.

1. Expected or obligated to give an account for something or someone; answerable; accountable; as, "He is responsible for the car."
2. Involving accountability, obligation, or duties; as, "He has a responsible position."
3. Answerable or accountable as being the cause, agent, or source of something; as, "Who is responsible for this state of affairs?"
4. Able to distinguish between right and wrong and to think rationally, and hence be accountable for one's behavior.
5. Able to pay debts or meet business obligations; trustworthy; dependable; reliable; as, "She is a responsible person."

In philosophical and in most in legal contexts, the primary sense has been number 4. We have wanted to know if we can hold people responsible for what they do. As our sense of being able to explain people's behavior has strengthened, we have been less inclined to hold people responsible for what they do. In this process we have omitted the effect of holding people morally accountable for their behavior. By no longer holding people to certain behavior we have dropped one major influence in getting them to behave in a manner supportive of the society.

Aristotle said we become just by doing justice, roughly speaking, we become moral by acting morally. We become brave by doing brave acts. We become morally responsible by being morally responsible. Aristotle and anyone who has ever had children or grandchildren would not believe moral behavior is natural in the sense that we are born to it. We have to train people to act morally by insisting upon certain behavior. We praise and blame, we morally commend and condemn to encourage and discourage certain behavior vital to the common interest. Strange as it may seem, we seem to have forgotten that in both the moral training of our children and in holding them and adults accountable for their actions. This is strange because we keep wondering why so many people fail to act morally.

But everything that happens in a society happens because someone has done it or is doing it. Good things we like and bad things we don't are done by one or more of us. What we do with others or even alone is our contribution to the complex of events we experience collectively in a society. The degree of responsibility each of us bears depends on how and where we are acting. We may be acting alone and in isolation or alone among others or with others in isolation or with others among others, as just one, as a couple, as a leader, as a member of a group, at a party, a crowd at a game, in religious observance, enrolled in a university, as a corporation board member, as a member of a government, army or police.

A common error is thinking it all right to do what one pleases "as long as it doesn't hurt anyone." What one does in private, for example, can have no consequences for anyone else and so it is nobody else's business. Most people of experience know that very little one does ever remains private. Think of how rarely secrets are kept and all of the ways they come to light. That, however, is not the error. The error is in looking too narrowly at what one is doing. Consider a man and a woman each married to someone else who have an affair. Think of the faithful spouses who begin to suspect their husbands or wives may be having an affair and how the suspicion undermines the basis of trust for their marriage vows and even for marriage as it is understood and cultivated in their society.

Suppose their spouses never do learn of the affair. No harm done? Possibly not, unless we consider implications their affair has for the affections they have toward their spouses. For example, does "living a lie" affect their ability to relate? But, more than that, an ethical society is based on trust that even in private one will do what one is expected to do, act responsibly, even when one can "get away" with not doing so. The decline of our sense of responsibility is serious because it goes to the very heart of morality, and yet we seem increasingly incapable of holding ourselves and others accountable. Why is this? There are many reasons. Consider some conspicuous ones.

Everyone is a "victim." No one is a cause of his socially unsatisfactory behavior. "Circumstances" or "someone else" made me do it. We see this in criminal law defenses. Lyle and Eric Menendez shot gunned their father and mother to death and nearly got away with it on the defense that one of the brothers was a victim of child abuse by his father and was in fear of being killed by his father who was watching television at the time he was shot. The defense that would win the prize if one were given for these is the one offered in the Harvey Milk murder. The killer who went into the San Francisco city hall with a loaded pistol and emptied it into Harvey Milk was acquitted on the defense that he had been eating Twinkies for several days causing his blood sugar to go awry and consequently was not responsible for the murder.

Doubtless, readers can add many of their own favorite such defenses and excuses. These illustrate the reluctance of juries to find people accountable for their action if they can possibly avoid it, and that is largely because of our lost sense of moral responsibility.

"Mistakes were made." But no one person or persons in particular made them. This suppression of responsibility is found commonly in organizations, especially in governmental bureaucracies. Mistakes were made, but there seems no way to find who made them or where. The use of the passive voice in memoranda and reports becomes moral displacement language. Congressional investigations reek with them. Sometimes scapegoats are hung out to dry, but only if moral equivalency language fails to baffle the investigators and bore the public into dropping the inquiry. As organizations grow more complex, it becomes increasingly difficult even for people of good will to find who is responsible for the socially undesirable behavior. Anyone who has tried to get fair treatment from a large corporation understands this well. Kierkegaard once remarked: "A crowd in its very concept is the untruth, by reason of the fact that it renders the individual completely impenitent and irresponsible, or at least weakens one's sense of responsibility by reducing it to a fraction."

"She couldn't help it." Something made her do it—her upbringing, her poverty, her strong feelings, her compassion, her social conditions. This is to offer a psychological or a sociological explanation instead of moral accountability. It is to see a person's action as coming from causes external to the person, as if the person himself had nothing to do with it, made no choice, no decision in the course of action he took. "We all lie," says one famous psychiatrist, as if that proves we shouldn't discourage ourselves and other from doing so. The famous trial lawyer, Clarence Darrow, favored this view of human action. He was fond of saying to juries in defense of his clients: "If you had been raised in the circumstances of the defendant and suffered the same upbringing, you would be the defendant." We all know this in the form, "There but for the grace of God go I." And on this view of human action there is no way we could hold a person morally responsible. The person's actions are determined.

"That's the way those people are." We cannot expect certain groups to live by our standards. "Mexican field hands will stab each other in bars." "Teenagers will be sexually active." "Boys will be boys." "Some people will use language in their songs some of us consider foul." This kind of thinking is pluralistic, bordering on relativism, but more likely a form of bigotry. Through their intolerance people who think this way write off whole sections of people as incapable of being responsible for their actions.

On the other side of the coin there are those Walker Percy calls the "super decent" and "super tolerant." They tolerate everybody because they "understand." They choose to be open-minded about how others behave because to do other is to be "judgmental." Consequently, anything goes. Since teenagers, for example, are going to have premarital sex, the only decent thing to do is to facilitate this for them lest we be considered prudes. Since we cannot cast the first stone, so to speak, we must not judge. What is amusing about these "open-minded" people is how close-minded they are toward others who do not think exactly like them. The person who "understands" others is the really decent human. The person who insists on responsibility is "moralistic" and uncaring.

Just how this thinking got loose is hard to say, but it could be the result of a misinterpretation of a teaching of Jesus. In Matthew Jesus says:

> Do not judge, or you too will be judged. For in the same way you judge others, you will be judged, and with the measure you use, it will be measured to you.

> Why do you look at the speck of sawdust in your brother's eye and pay no attention to the plank in your own eye? How can you say to your brother, 'Let me take the speck out of your eye,' when all the time there is a plank in your own eye? You hypocrite, first take the plank out of your own eye, and then you will see clearly to remove the speck from your brother's eye.[1]

The teaching is to make judgments on a standard you would apply to yourself and not to use a standard drawn from your own limited and perhaps distorted point of view. Do not judge until first you can see clearly. But this is not to say do not judge at all.

Likewise in John, we read:

> The teachers of the law and the Pharisees brought in a woman caught in adultery. They made her stand before the group and said to Jesus, "Teacher, this woman was caught in the act of adultery. In the Law Moses commanded us to stone such women. Now what do you say?" They were using this question as a trap, in order to have a basis for accusing him.

But Jesus bent down and started to write on the ground with his finger. When they kept on questioning him, he straightened up and said to them, "If any one of you is without sin, let him be the first to throw a stone at her." Again he stooped down and wrote on the ground.

At this, those who heard began to go away one at a time, the older ones first, until only Jesus was left, with the woman still standing there. Jesus straightened up and asked her, "Woman, where are they? Has no one condemned you?"

"No one, sir," she said.

"Then neither do I condemn you," Jesus declared. "Go now and leave your life of sin."[2]

This passage is filled with meaning for religion and for ethics. The content most relevant to contemporary confusion about moral responsibility lies in condemnation and forgiveness. The passage illustrates how foolish we are to judge others harshly when few, if any of us, were our conduct on the line, could escape similar judgment. Either the standard or the punishment is unrealistic or both are. The teaching is that a person is not to be condemned for bad conduct but not that bad conduct is not bad conduct. Otherwise the woman would not be commanded to go and leave her life of sin.

Note the absence of any reference to the male involved in the adultery. I cannot help wondering why he was not presented for stoning. There are, no doubt, historical explanations and explanations of the Mosaic Law that might account for his not being around.

If we are not given a chance to improve our behavior and are condemned the moment we breach a standard, we are not going to become responsible for our behavior. The teaching is that it is better for our growth and fulfillment if we are given a second chance. It is also better for the community if each individual learns to be responsible rather than for all of us to be conduct police for each other. The confusion is to think this means no one is really responsible because all is always forgiven. At some point the practice of forgiveness will either work or it won't. But it is useful always to distinguish between the unacceptable acts of a person and the person. Our censure should center on the wrong acts a person commits. The person should be encouraged not to do them again. A society which fails to do that fails to provide the possibility for growth of the individual.

Again, following Aristotle, we become moral by acting morally and being held accountable by others but especially by ourselves. We become moral by making informed decisions, balancing conflicting desires within ourselves, and our desires conflicting with those of others. We become moral, responsible selves, by engaging in operations of deliberation and choice. A morally good choice is one that is not an impulse or mere habit but a choice mediated by the exercise of intelligence. This takes practice and training. When we reflect how little training occurs in our present society, we should not be surprised at the ridiculous behavior we see depicted and cultivated in popular culture. Our upbringing affects our behavior, and we can expect very little of people who have not had proper training. But the answer does not lie in refusing to hold people accountable for their behavior. On the contrary, it is through holding people accountable that they become moral. This analysis shows just how critical moral training is to the proper functioning of a society and the well-being of the individuals who compose it.

The intelligent choices we make will also include choices regarding the welfare and integrity of the society. Choices we make without regard for our social existence impose upon the freedom of others in our society and eventually upon our own freedom. This is because we are, as individuals, and even as couples and groups, parts of a society. It is the failure to consider the welfare of others that debilitates and corrupts a society making it a mere collection of individual people grouped together on some arbitrary basis such as geographical location. To choose intelligently is to choose with regard to our social being; otherwise, we have missed a significant fact of our existence by not framing our choice properly. When we do take this fact into account, we are thinking morally. Every choice we make does not have moral implications, but any choice could have. For example, I may have two ounces of gun powder in my apartment, and that is my individual choice. But if I have 25 pounds of gun powder, then the potential for others in my building makes the matter a moral one.

Failure to recognize and teach this is our modern moral failure. We have failed to make clear the social character of our existence and to teach our successor generation to be responsive to it. Our failure does more than create social problems: it condemns the untrained to a shallow life of unknowing. Letting others off the moral hook is not doing them a favor. It is granting them half a life, a life devoid of responsibility, a life of ignorance of their actual existence. A person is held responsible in order to become responsible to the needs and claims of others with whom the person lives and upon whom the person depends for security and well being and who depend upon that person for theirs. We are each responsible to the explicit and implicit obligations in our positions in society. If we are not sensitive to them, we relegate ourselves to a lower social status or perhaps none at all.

A series of articles on teenagers and pregnancy appeared in *The Atlanta Constitution.*[3] The content is heartening to the moralist because it begins to put responsibility where at least half of it belongs—on the males who prey upon the young girls who get pregnant. The writer discusses the social myths about the subject, the girls who get pregnant, the boys who get them pregnant, how parents should advise their children, and who is dealing with the problem of teen pregnancy. This, too, is heartening because by the breadth of its coverage it recognizes a problem for the entire society. In discussing the role of males in the problem, the writer discusses paths leading to unexpected fatherhood. There is the "allure of sex," "being macho," "absent role models," "pop culture," and, behold, "no incentives for responsibility."

The incentives lacking are that boys under 18 who are full-time students are not required by the law to make child payments, the pregnant girls often do not force the issue, and regulations prevent a woman from receiving full Aid to Families With Dependent Children benefits with the father at home or working more than 100 hours a month. Conspicuously missing is reference to any moral responsibility the teenagers, both male and female, have and any moral responsibility the rest of society has toward them. Neither the teenagers nor the rest of us appear to have any moral responsibility. It is just a matter of what happens. One boy seems to have some grip on the matter. He says, "I'm always ready to help out my little girl. Some guys aren't man enough. But it takes two to make a baby. I made that baby." He is ready to help his girl at least, but he has no sense of helping society by not having the baby in the first place and, once having the baby, that he has a responsibility to care for it.

This attitude is further clarified by another boy. He is quoted as saying, "I want to go to college. I don't want to bring a child into this world, and I'm not ready to care for it. I'm not going to do anything to mess up my future." His thinking is commendable in many ways, but his focus is on his future alone, his duty to himself, so to speak, but to no one else. It would be better to include in his consideration his duty to society. Similarly, it would be better to include in the entire consideration the duty of society to him and all of the other poorly guided teenagers. The responsibility works both ways, them to us and we to them. It may be that the teenagers have little to anticipate in their lives and so little incentive to behave as we would want them to behave.

One incentive would be to meet their social responsibilities. If we are looking at causes of their behavior, we should include causing them to meet their social responsibilities. Boys and girls who create babies and drop them on society are not being morally responsible. They are imposing on our freedom. People who allow them to do that are not either because they are allowing the boys and girls to act in ways that limit their own freedom. To the extent we do not do that, when it doesn't even come into the discussion of a series of articles in a major city newspaper, we are in effect saying the teenagers have no responsibility to us nor we to them.

Again, one is held responsible in order to become responsible. Our failure to hold individuals in our society responsible to us for their behavior is our failure to take them seriously, to care about them, and our failure to expect them to care about us. And from this we can see that without any sense of obligation we should not even be willing to consider ourselves members of the same society.

Three final points will bring this chapter to a close. First, there is moral responsibility because we live intentionally in groups. What we decide to do may have a bearing on the lives of others. When it affects our life together, we are involved in matters of moral responsibility. Those who do not or will not consider others take themselves outside the society. Second moral responsibility is not resolvable into psychological or sociological facts. It cannot be derived by describing people acting in groups. It can only be recognized by each of us acting as a moral agent. That means we act as individuals recognizing our responsibility to others in our actions—what it is we intend in living together. Third, we must bring children into the society of morally responsible human beings. This is an educational process that does not occur spontaneously. We have to make it happen.

We do this by teaching children to make intelligent choices in light of the life they share in a society, a life of obligations to the rest of us and us to them. This is how we pass on our moral heritage, especially in a changing world wherein it is uncertain the way we have lived together in the past is the way we will be able to live in the future.

Notes

1. Matthew 7:1-5 NIV.
2. John 8:3-11 NIV.
3. Miriam Longino, "Teens and Pregnancy," *The Atlanta Journal/Constitution, January 14-18,* 1996.

Chapter IX

ℰ◯ℛ

Why Be Moral?
Steering Your Own Course

"He is free who knows how to keep in his own hands the
power to decide, at each step, the course of his life and
who lives in a society which does not block the exercise of
that power"

—Salvador de Madriaga

We have all been in situations where we knew what we ought to do
but were reluctant to do it either because we wanted to do something
else or because it required too much of us. Why do the right thing when
it costs us personally? Why try to find the owner of the Rolex watch you
just found on a restaurant table? Why risk personal injury to yourself to
help a person being mugged across the street? Why keep your marriage
vows when you can sleep with this person in secret? To answer these
questions and the dozens like them, we have to take account once more
the social nature of morality.

The person on a desert island has no moral responsibilities because
there is no one on the island with whom he is cooperating for his life. He
may recall interactions with others elsewhere and his relationships with
them. He may plan interactions with others elsewhere and his relationships

with those, too. He has none in his present condition. As an isolated person, morality is practically irrelevant to him. Morality is a societal matter. But suppose he is suddenly rescued and returned to civilization, his home town in Indiana. Does something have to happen before he can have any moral responsibilities? Is he without conscience in the meantime? These questions bring home what it is to be moral.

A person raised in the company of others who is able to live more or less in harmony makes choices and acts in a manner that will permit the harmony to continue. The person is acculturated. He will trust his fellow towns people to tell him the truth, respect his property, and his life, just as they will trust him. That way of behaving while living together is being moral. Whenever either he or any of them acts in such a way to break that trust, they are being immoral. If he or some others of them cannot act the right way, they are not acculturated. The society had a chance to bring them up right but, apparently, failed. So, the question, Why be moral? begins to look strange. It begins to look like one is asking, Why live a civilized life?

The question about being moral is confused. It suggests there is some other more sensible way to live, possibly a life of egoism or a life outside civilization. This may come from the common misinterpretation of Hobbes' social contract as a simple choice between being moral and not being moral. To live in peace and security, Hobbes argued, you enter the social contract by obeying the law of the absolute and undivided sovereign. For Hobbes life outside of society, in a state of nature, is intolerable. Each person who is endowed by the creator with natural rights hands over certain rights to a sovereign authority which in turn lays down a set of laws and makes each of us obey them.[1] But as useful as Hobbes' theory might have been for his political situation of the Seventeenth Century, it is not useful for the ethical situation of the Twentieth.

Even if we accept the idea of creator who endows us with natural rights and the idea of a social contract, we are still left with the question, Why be moral, or, as Hobbes would say, "obey the law," when we can get away with it? I'll come back to this question in a moment. But there is a greater weakness. Law and morality are related but nevertheless distinct. Law alone cannot provide the social order when no one can rely on anyone else to obey the law when not forced to do so. If I cannot rely on that, then why should I obey the laws when not forced? If each of us obeys the law only when forced, then what kind of state do we have?

Perforce it is one with an enforcer at everyone's elbow. Then who enforces the enforcers? In fairness, Hobbes does claim we each have to "internalize" the law and make it self-enforcing. My point, though, remains the same: without the threat of external enforcement, we would not bother to internalize the law.

Fortunately, modern philosophers can improve upon Hobbes. They can show that, while it is true that a mere contract cannot bring about the state of mutual trust directly from a state of nature where everyone is for himself, it is also true that most colonies of people already have mutual trust among themselves simply because there are established ways of doing things. Only in societies where there is some order are the conditions such that we can speak of morality at all.[2] As living persons we are interacting in a context where our actions are shaped by the way that context works. Being moral is not making a specific choice; it is understanding how one's society is supposed to work and acting in ways that make it work. Of course, one can "use" one's society, but others will not long permit that. I shall explain in a moment.

When my society expects me to do something I prefer not to do, it is rarely a simple matter. It involves my entire complex of relationships. If I am asked to risk my life in a war of national security, I do not ask merely if it is my duty and try to find some ethical theory to answer my question. Will my going bring about the greatest happiness for the greatest number? Is it commanded to me by God? Does my conscience dictate it? Rather, if I consciously pause to ask, I weigh a complex of factors bearing on me as a member of a human community: What would happen to my wife and children if I did not go to war? What would happen to my brother, his wife and children, and our neighbors? How would losing the war jeopardize my way of life? What will happen if I do go to war? Why am I called rather than others? Suppose nobody goes, or only a fraction of those needed to win? Is there some way other than fighting? Who takes care of the things at home we have been at pains to develop for our well-being?

Doing the right thing has for so long been looked upon as some one right choice one must make as if there is only one way to respond to situations. Moralists, in their wisdom, have tried to make things simple for us, to find the magic means of choosing. But anyone who has tried to counsel others in their choices knows that is not how it is. Moral questions are always difficult; otherwise, we would seldom ask them. Being moral is not some one thing, not some one way to act. It is doing whatever life with others for the sake of shared goals requires. Determining that is never easy. But the reason to be moral and act accordingly is that is what the life you are living requires.

Is it possible we are moral just by our nature, we do not have to have a reason to be moral but just are, we do what is right by our nature, by being human beings? Anyone who has raised children knows that cannot be true. We all know, even in ourselves we do not always do what we know we ought to do. We often have to fight our natural tendencies as we try to do what we think is right. That is one reason both Plato and Aristotle put so much emphasis on moral education and training.

Society enables you to realize the possibilities of your life. It makes life easier, by establishing patterns of behavior that keep things more or less settled, patterns built on trust. Mating, child rearing, commerce are made orderly and safe for you, giving you opportunities you would not otherwise have to use your talents and enjoy what there is in this life. These arrangements, however, are not without their cost in moral behavior expected from you. Since the arrangements are for the good of everyone alike, everyone should support them. Difficulties arise when there is less than general perception that they are for the good of everyone alike. It is rarely easy to get this universal perception, and this is what moral debate is about. But there is a rational basis upon which such debate can proceed: Is this action necessary for the sake of what we are doing together to benefit each of us?

Now let's go back and ask what keeps me from working the system? If most other people try to work together, then I can benefit from that and not really play by their rules. I can take two newspapers from the vending machine, keep one, and sell the other. To begin an answer, consider a society where we each seek only our own individual interest. Here we do whatever we want, and we refrain from doing whatever we want only when we think it may not be smart. For example, we may want to push the retail clerk in the face because he can't pull the telephone from his ear long enough to pay real attention to us. But there are laws against this, and possibly he is stronger than we are. So, we decide for our own good to be cool and wait for a pause in the clerk's conversation. This is the reasonable thing to do, anyway. Likewise for our other conduct in such a society. We will look out for ourselves, be careful crossing the street, eat reasonably, work to earn the money we need, and do the other things we think will "pay off" for us.

What happens when we need someone else's help to get some good things done for ourselves? Why should someone else help us? Well, we could try to "get him" to help us by "working around," cajoling, deceiving, intimidating, or strong arming him. We might even pretend to be very moral and decent humans, so he thinks we are like everyone else in the society who are cooperating for the common good. But if it becomes evident this is what we are doing, then we will find it harder and harder to get what we want. And if enough people begin to act like us, then everyone becomes suspicious, views the other as a rival for things we each want, and we all lose the chance to go for the things we can accomplish only by working together.

There are two ways to live—in a society where people trust one another and work together or in a crowd where people do not trust one another and cannot work together. Which way will you live? If you choose to live in a crowd, do not expect much from others. If you choose to live in a society, you will be expected and even required to check your self-interest from time to time because that is in the nature of things. You cannot have cooperation if everyone does everything he wants whenever he wants. We have been trying that in the United States, overemphasizing individual rights, and finding that it does not work. We are finding that we do not like looking over our shoulders in every hotel or restaurant parking lot, paying higher prices because of the costs inflicted on us by shoplifters, afraid to go to certain sections of our town, indeed, afraid even to be alone in our houses at night.

Again, living in a real society requires trust, the belief that I and everyone else does what together we need doing, even when I and everyone else can secretly get away with not doing it or doing something else in conflict with it. Maybe you or I could do better for ourselves by pursuing our own self-interest than by doing what is right, especially when others do what is right and observe established practices for the good of all. But then we are not being moral. We make ourselves liars because as members of a society we are forsworn to being moral. Is it reasonable to live as a member of society or in a mob waiting to happen? Is it reasonable to do our part to maintain the society? Could we do better as candidates for outcasts of elsewhere, outside the company of civilized people?

Now comes the cynic. "But what you say won't make me be moral." Of course not. It may not even motivate you to be moral. But it gives a rational basis for holding each of us who chooses to live in our society to account for our actions. And if we cannot account for our actions as socially permissible, then the members of the society we are pretending to join can so indicate and cast the shame that goes with it. If we have been properly nurtured, we will be remorseful, and if we are not, they will have to work on us to correct our defective upbringing and resultant attitudes. And if we do not like that, we can leave.

No amount of moral understanding will make people do what is right. But we are obliged to hold each of us to our responsibilities as each of us is obliged to hold ourselves to our responsibilities. Taking our responsibility and being held to our responsibility can influence our actions. But these reflections are not the cause of our moral behavior: they are the basis upon which we justly influence required moral behavior in each of us. In our so-called society today, we are not willing "to get involved" and hold others responsible for their conduct. This is a "free country." We do not hold one another responsible, and we assume we are not responsible.

Since we believe others are not being responsible to society, we doubt we should be. We look out for ourselves. We do what we "feel" is right. We say that morality is a "personal" matter. We act like artists who no longer know what artists should do so they make up something to do and try to make it "interesting." Sometimes it is interesting, but without reference to reality the interest dies as soon as something else "more interesting" comes along. And without reference to the company of civilized people, what is it to keep one's own morality? Is it to watch out for oneself, keep out of trouble, stay out of other people's way? This is not my actual choice as long as I choose to be among people who do go out of their way to create and secure the civilized life I enjoy. There is a price for it. If I am exempt, why not others, and if so, who will they be? Does it even make sense to say morality is a personal, an individual matter? How could it be? Trying to make it so makes moral life impossible.

There is reason to be moral, and if anyone is to be moral, then we all have to be. If we all have to be moral, then each person has to be. If we want others to be moral, then each of us has to be. The cynic says, "Tell that to them." The cynic wants something stronger than a rational analysis showing how it all makes sense for each and every one of us to be moral. The cynic wants to hear something to make him be moral, something compelling or even coercive, something more than sweet reason.

Recently, there has been a great deal of attention devoted to moral training, the lack of it, and ways to go about it. This is an important and encouraging development. For decades it has been ignored and is now nearly a lost art. Following Aristotle, contemporary writers have focused on training such as would make us virtuous, ingrain in us traditionally admired moral behavior.[3] This way we would not just rationally decide but be psychologically compelled to do the right thing. This, presumably would restore morality to us. One could hardly argue against doing this. But training alone will not restore morality. There was plenty of this kind of moral training in the past, maybe even too much. Morality will be aground until a general population recognizes the need for it and sets it afloat again.

The call to morality for us living at the beginning of the Twenty-first Century can only be heard as a distant cry. Though we have experienced two world wars, a hosts of other major armed conflicts, and the Cold War, we have also experienced the most substantial advances for mankind in all of history. The advances have been largely material and technical, but they have provided us with almost fantastical powers of control over our world and a sense of power over our individual lives. We have shivered at the thought of all out atomic war. We have been terrified by the prospect of one of us or our loved ones developing a serious illness, and terrorized by the prospect of bombs in our passenger airplanes. But, our material well-being has given us an illusion of individual self-sufficiency, an illusion of total freedom.

This makes the call to morality so faint to our ears. Having traveled widely, I have always been impressed by the generosity of the poor. I have been shamed by it. I recall a time when I stopped my car to rest on a remote mountain top in Greece. One of those many wayside shrines found in such places caught my attention. As I walked to it, I noticed a man selling candies and beckoning to me. Choosing to be polite and not ignore him, I mustered up my best Greek to explain I didn't want to buy anything. He said he didn't care and just wanted to give me some candy for my refreshment. That turned out to be true, to my very pleasant surprise. I was reminded of seeing in other countries Moslems, practically beggars themselves, offer in charity some of their meager resources to others.

Two or three years later at a dinner party I met a young woman who had just returned from humanitarian service in a village of poor people in India. I told her of my experiences of the kindness of poor people. She said she had seen the same thing. I asked her if she got to know the people well enough during her two years there to guess why. She said she thought it was because they lived so closely together and depended so much upon one another and there was no one and nothing else. Strange as this may sound, I find this enviable. With the material wealth of the Western World and the rare encounter of such poverty, it is easy to forget we owe one another for what we have. "Nobody ever gave me anything, and I don't owe anybody anything," cries the cynic. Think of how you feel when one of those "other people" helps push your car out of the snow. And what about the design of the car and the construction of the road? The point is not to shame us into being moral through sentimentality for the poor. It is only to indicate we are missing something.

To understand this better, consider the philosopher Immanuel Kant. In a little understood aspect of his work on ethics he hints at a reason to be moral that may be persuasive to us in the Twenty-first Century precisely because of our sense of mastery of ourselves and our world. In Kant's ethical theory he presents the idea of the Categorical Imperative. Put briefly it is whenever you are deciding what is right, choose that action whose maxim you could will to become a universal law of nature. The maxim is what you would say is the meaning of the act. For example, you have promised to meet your friend for dinner at the restaurant where you both enjoy dining. On your way there you meet another, closer friend, and you decide you would enjoy dinner better with that person at another restaurant and do so, thereby breaking your promise.

Kant would say that the maxim of your action was as follows: "When you have made a promise and find it inconvenient to keep it, you don't. Now try to make that a universal law, so you can expect everybody would do that. You can see this would be a self-defeating law. The immediately plausible explanation is that breaking one's promise would be imprudent because it would weaken the socially valuable practice of promising. But that was hardly Kant's point. He was not exactly worried about what was socially valuable. Rather, he was saying it is contrary to reason for a person to make such a promise because he did not really intend to keep it, or because he would keep it only if it were convenient which is about the same thing. If everybody broke any promise the moment it became inconvenient to keep it, one would not really be making promises. In short a lying promise is logically incoherent.

Most people can grasp even this quite abstract rationale for keeping promises. But this takes us only part of the way. To get to a vision of what it means to be moral, we must consider Kant's alternative vision of his Categorical Imperative. This he calls the Kingdom of Ends. In this Kingdom we observe one rule: treat people only as ends, never solely as means. We have a common sense ethical notion very much like this when we say things like "He uses people," or "You are not interested in me but in what I can do for you." Applied to promises this rule says, "Don't tell a person you will meet him in order to keep him on the hook for you in case you can't find something better to do." Why not? Because you are manipulating the person to please yourself, getting him to do something he would not do on his own if he knew the truth and did not trust you as he does.

What is wrong with that? That is making a slave of the other person. But that is not the worst part: you are making a slave of yourself by failing to dwell in the Kingdom of Ends where you and not your spontaneous desires are in control. The self actualizes itself when it controls its desires to some purpose. Only when we are not slaves to desire are we free to do as we will and be fully human. Likewise, when someone treats us that way, deceives us to get us to do what he desires with no real intention of keeping his word, we are not free. We are being used. And when we treat others that way, we are using them.

Being moral is our opportunity to act with control and focus and to experience our freedom at the highest level. Alternatively, we dissipate ourselves by riding off in a thousand different directions chasing inconsistent desires. Today we have come to think of morality and freedom in stark contrast. The last half of the Twentieth Century was a time of revolt against Victorian manners and morals, freedom from the restraints of narrowly moralistic doctrines, indeed freedom from any and all doctrine. As a result, personal freedom has become widely interpreted as license and nonchalance.

In fact, we have to make choices or lose control of our lives. Reality does not allow each of us an infinite variety of options, and each of us is subject to a host of conditions internal and external to our selves according to which we must make our choices. The person who acts capriciously is frivolous and weak-willed, letting life take him where it will. The person who acts with deliberation, intelligence, and resolve controls one's life as much as is possible. In learning, judging, and choosing one becomes free, that is, an autonomous self capable of finding life meaningful. The free individual realizes that others are similarly free and recognizes their freedom as significant because it has been mainly through interaction with others the individual has become free. Others have loved him, supported him, taught him, and most of all have not tread upon him or his dreams and allowed him to live a fulfilled life.

Modern thinking has been just the opposite: it has concluded that the only way to be free is to stop caring about "what other people may think" and that one can only do "one's thing" by being willing to run over others or not caring about them. But we are not born with freedom; we achieve it through spiritual development in a context we inherit from our society of family, friends, and the totality of our fellow freedom seekers. Only in a society, with institutions and moral practices developed for the sake of individual freedom can we each achieve freedom, and only by doing our part, respecting its members, recognizing their freedom, these institutions and practices, in short, being moral, can we be assured of the best chance for our own.

The ultimate immorality is conduct violating what we have put in place to facilitate the freedom of each of us in society. The person who does not ask what bearing his conduct has on others is not a person of good will and is on the verge of acting immorally. Similarly, institutions and practices inhibiting our progress toward freedom are themselves immoral and need revision or rejection. Returning the Rolex watch, limiting or redirecting one's desires from time to time to avoid clashes with the desires of others assures that others will do the same for you. Being moral is lending one's effort to the total social atmosphere in which everyone's freedom prospers.

It is not always easy to see how or whether one's actions add or detract. It is usually easy to avoid looking deeply into one's situation and ignore one's social responsibilities. But the obligation is present nevertheless, and those who do not examine their actions to see what social bearing they have we call self-centered and maybe even selfish. They are people who do not do their part, but they enjoy the freedom to ignore the rest of us because we are doing our part. That is not right because our greatest occasion of freedom is when other people's desires do not keep us from fulfilling ours. Taking the property of another when we desire it makes it impossible to enjoy one's own property. Holding great amounts of property makes it impossible for others to have any.

This is how living morally in a moral society allows us to direct the course of our own lives rather than having others do it for us. So, contrary to what people commonly think, morality, does not limit our freedom, it assures it. The moments of happiness we must forego to support morality means we do not have happiness forced upon us as conformity to some ideal prescribed by others. We are sustaining our freedom by keeping out of the way of others and others doing the same for us. The result is harmony that promotes a diversity of choice wherein we can seek and enjoy what is fulfilling to each of us. As noted before, if being happy were all there was to living, more mood elevating drugs would be the answer. But fulfilling our desires through a refinement of judgment and choice determines our moral destiny.

Will this explanation make people be moral? No, but it is a reason for each of us to keep trying to be and to keep urging others to be.

Notes

1. Thomas Hobbes, *Leviathan,* New York, Oxford University Press, 1947, pp. 100-2; 132ff.
2. Kurt Baier, *The Moral Point of View,* Random House, 1965, pp. 118-20.
3. See, for example, William J. Bennett (ed.), *The Book of Virtues*, New York, Simon & Schuster, 1993 and similar efforts by William Bennett and others.

Chapter X

ಬಿಂ

Moral Literacy: Knowing the Ropes

". . . it is so easy to be wrong—and to persist in being wrong—when the costs of being wrong are paid by others."—Thomas Sowell

Moral literacy is knowing how morality applies to contemporary life. While understanding morality does not guarantee one will be moral, not understanding morality does guarantee one will find little use for it. Moral literacy is no less serious than mathematics, scientific, or computer literacy. In the pragmatic culture of our times one would never know it. But think of how much effort goes into training people to calculate profits and how little into training people to generate them fairly and honestly. Who cares, as long as you are earning more? Can you count on that without some attention to moral literacy? Think of what it costs a business to be seen as dishonest to its clients or unfair to its employees. Look at some of the common views on morality and what is wrong with them.

1. *"Business Ethics is an Oxymoron."*

Cynicism about business is deeply entrenched. Unfortunately expecting so little from business practice helps assure little can be expected. But ethics bears upon business in numerous ways.

First, there is an ethical way to do business. The cynicism creeps in because selling is always involved. A customer is invited to buy. How this is done may be ethical or unethical. A customer may be treated as means or ends. If treated as means, then the seller tries to "get" the customer to buy. The seller uses the customer to make a sale. If treated as ends, the seller tries to discover what the customer's need is and to supply that need. The interest of both buyer and seller are met, and the transaction is ethical.

Related to this is honesty with regard to the product or service offered. If the seller provides the buyer the product he needs, then the buyer's interest is being met. But if the product is not what the buyer needs, then the buyer is being deceived, and that is not ethical. So there is an ethical way of doing business, for a profit, yes, but also by being honest, treating one another with respect. Business is not unethical, but the way it is practiced may be. Business people should be held to the same ethical standards as anyone else.

Second, business operates in a society only because it is good for that society. As soon as it becomes deleterious to the society, it is no longer needed. Businesses can be good and bad for society in many ways. One way it can be good is by contributing to the economic well-being of the society by providing goods and services at fair prices otherwise not available. One way it can be bad is by providing goods or services at unfair prices that people cannot do without and are thereby exploited.

Third, owners and managers can treat their employees ethically or not and employees can treat their owners and managers ethically or not, and workers can treat one another ethically or not. Sometimes, and increasingly, they do not. There is sexual harassment and employment discrimination. There is on-the-job conflict because workers with different backgrounds disagree about how to do their jobs. Some people think you have to be extremely punctual arriving; others extremely punctual leaving. Some like music; some do not. Some like loud music; some like soft. Some like to tell jokes of a certain sort; other do not. If there are office rules, they require interpretation. When is music too loud? When is one staff member's expression of interest in another romance and when is it sexual harassment? Do the rules tell?

Business may present us situations where we may be tempted to do what we would not do at home or in our neighborhood because we did not think it right. We might never consider cheating the milkman or the paper boy because there are never more than a few dollars at stake in our transactions with them. But with multi-million dollar contracts and thousands of dollars in bribes directed our way or a major promotion for us if we succeed and offering a bribe could assure we succeed, we might just be tempted. With the authority over the continued employment, salary increases, and promotions of an attractive member of your staff, you might just expect a few sexual favors. With the subtle cooperation of fellow workers you might just create an atmosphere that makes an attractive coworker go along with some sexual shenanigans you wouldn't really dare on your own.

These are not moral mysteries of the world of business. They are immoral behavior. Cheating in our dealings with others is clearly a form of dishonesty. Sexual harassment is clearly a form of coercion and barely different from other methods of seeking sex through force. Indeed, any forcing of responses from others is failure to respect their individual freedom, a fundamental moral error.

There is an ethical resolution of these "situations." What interest do the conflicted parties share? It is a satisfactory working environment. It is in the interest of each employee, the management, and even the customers. It is not as if no one knows this, nor as if no one knows how he or she is supposed to behave. The puzzles appear when people play dumb and a third party tries to lay out rules to follow. Put the conflicted parties together, and let them work out the conflict. They will because they live in families and communities. They just need to be called to account. That is what is missing in contemporary working environments, schools, and communities. No one in any of these contexts would say it is good to bother one another or there is nothing anyone can do to avoid bothering one another. Business is no exception. The moral illiteracy of using the literary term "oxymoron" is in absolving people in business of moral responsibility.

2. *"Honesty is the Best Policy."*

This bit of moral illiteracy is closely related to the preceding one. Many business people say honesty is the best policy, and they seem to think that is enough. Being honest to your customers is good for business, and if it's good for business, then it's good, period. If you are dishonest to a customer, she might find out and not come back or, even worse, sue you. So, really, it pays to be honest. But what happens when it doesn't pay? Unless you believe it always pays to be honest, no matter what, then if you think it will pay you to be dishonest, you will be dishonest, that is, modify your policy. Suppose you have a warehouse full of computer printers you bought at great discount. You discover they tend to break down after a few months use. If you tell your customers, they will not buy them. If you cannot sell them, you will go broke. You know you can sell them, sell out, and clear out of town before customers find out the printers are poorly made. What is your policy now?

There are, of course, many possible scenarios. You could inform your customers about the defect and offer a service warranty or offer the printers at an extremely low price. But what if the only way to avoid going broke is just to say nothing, sell, and clear out of town? Honesty is not a matter of policy but of ethics. If it is wrong to lie, it is not because it doesn't pay but because it undermines business. A society does not tolerate lying business people because they thwart rather than facilitate the activities of the society. Again, honesty is required of business people, not because it is the best policy for them, but because it is the best policy for the society. It is not for business people to decide when or when not to be honest; it is decided for them if they want to do business in the society. Here we can see the fallacy in the morally illiterate phrase "business ethics" suggesting a special kind of ethics for business different from ethics for the rest of us. If a business cannot operate honestly as all of us understand honesty, then it doesn't need to operate.

3. *"That's What Sells. It's What People Want."*

This line of moral illiteracy has become very popular. Movies and television are particularly given to this self-serving fallacy: you can't hold them accountable for the taste and expectations of the people in their markets. After all, they are in business to make money. You can't expect them to give up profit and offer content that doesn't sell, can you? Yes, you can. The media have as much social responsibility as the rest of us. To operate in our society, they must live by the same standards the rest of us do. Trying to make money does not make them less accountable than the rest of us.

The debate often takes a freedom of speech form. This has for most of the last century served the media well. Because it is difficult for the courts to draw lines about content the media have had rather easy sway. But they can go too far. They have in seeking stories about the private lives of individuals. They have in depicting violence and other socially reprehensible things. When they do, we call them to account, and, for a while at least, they respond. Certainly they have in how they depict race and mental illness. They can continue to do more; provided we do not subscribe to the illiteracy that if it sells, if it's what the people want, it's okay.

Which people wants this stuff that sells, in their considered opinion? The argument would be about whether the public is really unwitting about what it is seeing and hearing. It would also be about whether the moral standards of the society are being met. When discussing mass media, it is not clear whose moral expectations we are talking about. If a national network broadcast goes to millions of individuals throughout the country, then which society are we talking about? Most countries are complexes of subcultures. But, more important, a media feed is a feed to that person as an individual and not as part of a community. The expectations of a moral society hardly comes into play. The media are quite free to call forth their own electronic communities.

The favorite defense is innocence. "We are just entertainers." This is hardly credible. The media control the images we see. They juxtapose ideas in ways they want us to see them, often with little rational content to justify them. If they want an auditorium to look empty, they can keep panning the empty seats. If they want it to look full, they can focus on the front row. If they want certain politicians, criminals or drug addicts to be fashionable, they can glamorize them. They are not mere bystanders in the values they present. If the media do not have persuasive force, why do sponsors pay millions of dollars for expensive commercials when a simple informational advertisement to let the public know about their product would do? The point here is, not to revisit the many ways the media make moralists unhappy, but to say if the media have axes to grind, they are in a position to grind them effectively. Even if they do not, the fact they stimulate interest in viewers suggests they may be serving their commercial interest at least as much as serving the interest of the society wherein they operate. So it is egregious moral illiteracy to say, "If it sells, it's okay." The seller must be aware of the social responsibilities of selling.

4. *"Everybody Does It, So It's Okay if I Do It."*

Parents hear this often from children. People who cheat on their income tax and other things say this. First, in most cases everybody doesn't do it. How would one know this, anyway? Saying it is usually an excuse to avoid doing what one ought to do. Second, what people do is not the criterion of what one ought to do. The criterion of what is right is what contributes to the common purpose of the people. Others may not do what they should because they do not understand that purpose or because they are not being responsible. It is not always easy to do either, but moral navigators try. Third, this illustrates the importance of trust in ethics. Thinking others are not being honest when unobserved, undermines one's own resolve to be honest when unobserved. This is the element most moral illiterates miss.

When there is no authority figure, no vengeful deity, no judge, no police, why be moral? That is the only way morality will work. So if you want a moral order to live in, you have to do what is moral, even when you are not made to do it, and so does everyone else. Of course, once everybody really does do it, you had better assess your position. Unless you think you, by your example of sticking to the right way, might turn things around and get others to do what is right, you should look for another way. In the company of liars, telling the truth would be pointless. You could not expect the truth from them, and even if you told them the truth, they would think you were lying.

5. *"Ethics is a Set of Rules Whereby You Determine What is Right and What is Wrong."*

This is a common error, born of the fond hope of making life simple. But no set of rules will "do it all" when it comes to ethics, not even the Ten Commandments. We are commanded to honor father and mother, and to keep the Sabbath holy. Suppose father's ox falls into a ditch on the Sabbath and is in danger of dying without immediate rescue and father asks us to do the rescue for him. We need to interpret the two relevant commandments. What will guide us? We have to keep asking ourselves what it is we are trying to accomplish with these rules. They are at best guidelines. When followed by and large, they tend to fulfill our purpose, but not always. This is obvious in "Always tell the truth." Suppose two thugs enter your house to kill your spouse who is hiding in the attic. They ask you if your spouse is in the attic.

There was no rule for Abraham Lincoln to follow. He said:

> I am called upon to assume the Presidency at a time when eleven of our sovereign states have announced their intention to secede from the Union, when threats of war increase in fierceness from day to day.

It is a grave duty which I now face. In preparing for it, I have tried to inquire: what great principle or ideal is it that has kept this Union so long together? And I believe that it was not the mere matter of separation of the colonies from the motherland, but that sentiment in the Declaration of Independence which gave liberty to the people of this country and hope to all the world. This sentiment was the fulfillment of an ancient dream, which men have held through all time, that they might one day shake off their chains and find freedom in the brotherhood of life. We gained democracy, and now there is the question of whether it is fit to survive.

Perhaps we have come to the dreadful day of awakening, and the dream is ended. If so, I am afraid it must be ended forever. I cannot believe that ever again will men have the opportunity we have had. Perhaps we should admit that, and concede that our ideals of liberty and equality are decadent and doomed. I have heard of an eastern monarch who once charged his wise men to invent him a sentence which would be true and appropriate in all times and situations. They presented him the words, "And this too shall pass away."

That is a comforting thought in time of affliction— "and this too shall pass away." And yet—let us believe that it is not true! Let us live to prove that we can cultivate the natural world that is about us, and the intellectual and moral world that is within us, so that we may secure an individual, social and political prosperity, whose course shall be forward, and which, while the earth endures, shall not pass away. . . .

I commend you to the care of the Almighty, as I hope that in your prayers you will remember me. . . . Good-bye, my friends and neighbors.[1]

The Union was divided on what was right. Lincoln had to find what was moral and to pursue it as indeed he did. Some people would call it a political decision; some an historical one. It may have been both, but it was primarily a moral decision because it was based on the purpose he found all Americans had as a common interest. It would not have done for him to refer to the divine right of kings which might have done for a European nation about to split. He had to find it for the American people. He could have referred to the economic interest of everybody, but that wouldn't work either. It had become a moral matter: each side was willing to pay the economic price because each side thought it was morally right.

It was a moral dispute, and that's why Lincoln had to have a moral answer.

Finding what is right is not a matter of checking the rules. It would be nice if it were. It takes experience and the wisdom gained from it. It also takes a person seeking to do what is right, in contrast to what is politically advantageous, or economically beneficial. So there is often a creative element in finding what is right. I say often and not always because for most of the small stuff we do not have to sweat. We can usually go by some rule that has worked toward the common interest in the past. "Always tell the truth." "You should keep your promises." But we all know that our real moral dilemmas aren't like that. The existentialists even held that one has to create rightness from the situation one is facing. One chooses and lives by one's choice. If one chooses to be a murderer, one must act by that choice and live with the consequences. It is as if no one else is around or matters, only you. The trouble with that is no one ever is alone, and so the choices one makes must flow from and contribute to the life and experience one has in common with others.

6. "Might Makes Right. What is Right is What the Rich, Powerful, and Famous Say it is."

It follows from this bit of moral illiteracy that Hitler was right to undertake the "final solution" and try to kill all Jews because he had the power to do it. On an individual scale it follows that it is right for a bully to coerce a weakling to do whatever the bully wants. This is not what we mean by "right." It seems this bit of moral illiteracy, too, is born of cynicism: it doesn't do any good to make claims of right against those who will not hear them and have the strength to coerce you to do their will. But ethics is about people who listen to one another because they want to accomplish things together. Nothing in ethics forces you to do what is right. It only lets you know. Getting people to do what is right is showing them their incentive to keep the society going.

7. "Ethics is a Matter of Conscience. I Know What is Right Because My Conscience Tells Me."

Literary fiction can tell us about life. In chapter 16 of Mark Twain's *The Adventures of Huckleberry Finn*, Huck is helping his slave friend Jim in a run for freedom from Miss Watson, Jim's owner. Huck and Jim are completing their raft journey down the Mississippi River, and just as they are getting to the place where Jim will be legally free, Huck has these thoughts:

> Jim said it made him all over trembly and feverish to be so close to freedom. Well, I can tell you it make me all over trembly and feverish, too, to hear him, because I begun to get it through my head that he was most free—and who was to blame for it? Why, me. I couldn't get that out of my conscience, no how nor no way. It hadn't ever come home to me, before, what this thing was that I was doing. But now it did; and it stayed with me, and scorched me more and more. I tried to make out to myself that I warn't to blame, because I didn't run Jim off from his rightful owner; but it warn't no use, conscience up and say, every time: "But you knowed he was running for his freedom, and you could a paddled ashore and told somebody." That was where it pinched. Conscience says to me: "What had poor Miss Watson done to you, that you could see her nigger go off right under your eyes and never say one single word? What did that poor old woman do to you, that you could treat her so mean?. . ." I got to feeling so mean and so miserable I most wished I was dead.

According to our conscience, Huck is doing the right thing helping Jim. According to Hucks's, he is doing the wrong thing. Even though he is very sympathetic to Jim, Huck thinks he is being morally weak not turning in Jim. Growing up in nineteenth century rural Missouri, where slave owning was the accepted practice, Huck's conscience tells him turning in Jim for trying to run away is the right thing to do. Thus, it is good to follow conscience, but only if it is based on proper moral reflection as Abraham Lincoln did so well.[2]

8. "If it Doesn't Hurt Anybody, it's Okay."

This is the "consenting adults" line of reasoning. It is made to appear sound as an ethic by not looking into just what "it" is. You find $100 on a busy street in a large city. Is it all right to take it for your own? Anyway, you can't find who lost it. You can pick it up and put it in your pocket without anyone really noticing. Well, what harm is done? If you don't think about the person who lost the money, then none. If you don't think about the value of having lost property returned, then none. If you and everybody at least try to return lost property, you can help create something good together.

What used to be called illicit sex usually gets this moral rationalization, mainly because it is usually had in private and others do not or are not supposed to know about it. Consider the following:

> John and Mary were happily married in a traditional ceremony. They spoke the usual vows and pledged to be faithful to each other, for richer or for poorer and in sickness and in health. All went swimmingly for about six years, until Mary was swept off her feet by Lorenzo, a talk show host she met at a business convention. Mary, too, is a media person. The convention was in Chicago. Mary and John live in Los Angeles. Lorenzo lives in New York. Lorenzo and Mary were lonesome, missing their spouses, got to talking, one thing led to another, and they landed in bed in Lorenzo's hotel room. They found this very pleasant and didn't attend many meetings, so no one noticed them or what they were doing. Since each is married, this was their secret. Nobody else would know, and that way nobody would be hurt. This would be a convention romance, and that was that. They never saw each other again.

Basing the moral assessment of their conduct on the "if it doesn't hurt anyone. . ." line, they believe they did nothing wrong. Did they? Even if you don't consider the promise Mary made to John and the mockery her action makes of promising, there is still the question of what that does to Mary's sense of her own integrity and trustworthiness. And consider John's trust of Lorenzo, whom he has not met but who is a member of civilized society. John should be able to trust Lorenzo, an adult male in his society, to respect the institution of marriage. Suppose Lorenzo didn't know Mary was married. Did he do anything wrong? He failed to assure that sexual conduct take place in his society in orderly ways. Naive, you say. Most certainly, but his conduct is immoral nonetheless.

9. *"The Right Choice is the One that Makes You Happy."*

This is so practically useless that it is a piece of moral ignorance. It takes so much for granted. It assumes what will make one happy will be consistent with the life one wants to live among other people. Suppose it makes one happy to fondle children sexually. The statement assumes something like this is not what makes you happy, and that means you are already making moral decisions on some basis other than or at least in addition to your pursuit of happiness.

The other problem with this is the notion of happiness itself. What is being happy? Is it being slap happy, or going around feeling pleased about something, yourself, or everything in general? "I just want to be happy." "Why can't people just be happy?" What makes happiness the ultimate moral pursuit? Can we each pursue it no matter what? Was the Nazi pursuit of happiness a good thing? The seductive thing about happiness is not that it implies a life of pleasure, but that it is a blanket term for "getting what I want." So choosing what makes you happy is choosing the good life. The only trouble is knowing what the good life is.

10. "In Deciding What is Right, Do What Creates the Greatest Happiness for the Greatest Number of People."

This is a statement of the classic ethical position known as Utilitarianism. Any mother who has tried to please her whole family during the holidays knows right away what is wrong with this. Most people don't know what will make them happy. You can make some happy, but only at the cost of making others unhappy, very unhappy, and even a few extremely unhappy. Imagine trying to do this for the whole society. Also, the same problems apply to trying to make everybody happy that apply to trying to make yourself happy. So you need to know the socially acceptable way to happiness. Then you don't add anything by repeating the utilitarian principle. The problem is finding just what that is.

The biggest problem with this idea appears in its dumbing down effect. It is being tried in schools, in politics, and most emphatically in the mass media. As you try to please more and more people, you have to appeal to lower and lower tastes, experiences, and aspirations. This is the opposite of self-realization.

11. "The Private Life of Any Public Figure is Nobody's Business."

Maybe those who say this have had their fill of hot stories about political leaders, some stories true, some highly doubtful. Maybe, too, it's because favorite idols keep getting smashed. Speaking of idols, we shouldn't forget sports figures and entertainers who like the spotlight on their private lives, in fact, thrive on getting things told on them. Lately, things have gone too far, even for some of them. What is too far? Probably when prying into their private lives makes it impossible for them to live their lives. Also, it has become a media sport trying to ruin someone because of some past indiscretion most mature people, even highly moral people, can understand and forgive.

Probably, the most serious reason someone says it's nobody's business is the belief that in government, at least, we should choose our leaders by how well they can lead us and not by what they do or don't do in their private lives. This is saying no matter what a person is like in private, we can still tell if he can do a good job as a leader by his public image. It is also saying, no matter what a person is really like in private, it has no bearing on his or her ability to lead. And, indeed, there have been leaders with less than perfect moral characters who have been effective. But can we say their private lives are always totally irrelevant to their duties as leaders?

We can if we think a leader is some kind of specialist with certain skills in getting legislation passed or managing a staff, a kind of technician. But is that what a leader is? A society is made of free individuals and subject to stresses and strains, many unanticipated. We want leaders who can withstand those stresses and strains better than the rest of us. That takes strength of character. We examine the leader's character to judge whether he or she will be able to endure the challenges we face, those before us now, those yet to come, and those leaders of lesser character will try to sweep under the rug because addressing them will be unpopular.

In the 1988 United States presidential election, both candidates knew about the savings and loan crisis and that the American taxpayers would have to pay for it. Neither candidate mentioned the crisis as a matter to be addressed. Well, of course. What would you expect? It would be political suicide to do so. Perhaps a leader cannot tell all. But which is better—a person who will do his utmost to reveal as much as he can or a person unwilling to risk it for selfish reasons? That's why we seek leaders of sound character. We want people giving the orders and setting the direction who are best able to do what ought to be done in face of difficulties we all experience in our life together. In soft times it is easy to play ostrich and say character does not matter.

We are not going to have all of the information of state, and we are not going to want it all. We entrust our leaders with it. If our leaders are not of sound character, they will make themselves look good and not tell us what is really happening. Will we know they are deceiving us? Not necessarily. The best historians have difficulty determining that and evaluating the performance of leaders even after years of research. Consider how little we know after years of investigation who was responsible for American lack of readiness at Pearl Harbor, who assassinated President Kennedy or Reverend Martin Luther King, Jr. The public face of our leaders is not sufficient for choosing them. We have to be as sure as we can that the leaders are people of sound character. We have to be as sure as we can, for example, that their ego needs are not such as to get us into a show off war. What better way to judge this than how the candidate conducts himself when not before the television cameras?

It is not as if government has no bearing on our moral life. In an era when government funds and regulates practically every aspect of our lives, there is no way to omit the moral conduct of those elected to run the government. We play a game on this saying the elected official is sworn to carry out the law regardless of his own morality. I will not say this is impossible, but I will say it makes one skeptical that an official of dubious moral character will be vigorous in his development and execution of laws with moral bearing. For example, an elected official who uses drugs privately, not in the remote past, but currently, can hardly be taken seriously when he says drug use in our society must be prohibited. An elected official's private life is not always relevant; but it is not always irrelevant either.

Certainly a leader's moral character is no less relevant than ours. To say the private life of our political leaders is irrelevant is to say we just don't care about moral living ourselves. Why should leaders be any less accountable to society in their private lives than the rest of us? Indeed, as leaders in the public eye their character is usually considered exemplary. If our society has a sound morality, then it is not too much to expect the leader to do his part to sustain our morality.

12. "Sincerity and Honesty are What Count. When You Get Right Down to it, All of the Rest of Morality is Just so Much Hypocrisy."

This is the moral stuff of current movies and television situation comedies. It is love conquers all because the people who "really care" triumph over the narrow moralistic bigots of our society, people who concentrate on conventional morality and don't consider human feelings.

And so it goes. Surely anyone who has thought enough about the fragility of our fleeting life has wondered why we should be sticklers about the details of morality. Why not loosen up a little and feel good about doing it? The moral illiteracy here is thinking we don't have to balance the quest for a little happiness against the quest for an ordered society in which that happiness can be attained.

When and how often do we forgive and forget the many moral transgressions that we humans so characteristically make? When do we drop the hypocrisy and the moral stringencies causing it and start to "understand" one another? Should things be like they were fifty years ago when the social disgrace of being an unwed mother could lead a girl to suicide? Of course not. But it does not follow that premarital pregnancies are okay because no provision is made to secure the nurture and love the child needs to become a contributing member of society. Here, as in most moral illiteracy the error is in focusing too narrowly on the issue. It is easy to feel sorry even for the perpetrator of the most heinous crime when he is incarcerated alone and afraid about what will become of him. We can evaluate actions morally only after we consider the implications the actions have for our society.

Sidney Biddle Barrows, relates in *Mayflower Madam*[3] some of the planning that went into "Cachet" her now famous call girl operation in Washington, D.C., as she remarks:

> . . . even if our honesty resulted in a little less business, we wouldn't lie to our clients. If a man called and asked whether the girl we were describing was beautiful—and she wasn't—we would say so: "No, I wouldn't call her beautiful. But she's really quite attractive, and she has gorgeous eyes." If the client asked specifically for a girl who was tall, blond, and busty, and nobody fit the bill, we would say, "I'm terribly sorry, but we don't have a girl with all of these qualities who's available right now. But Carolyn has beautiful blond hair, or if you'd like to see somebody tall, Shawna is a delightful redhead."[4]

As if people aren't supposed to be honest with one another in the first place, we are, presumably, to give moral credit to the Mayflower Madam for her "honesty."

That her "honesty" was based on the business consideration that this practice would pay off financially in the long run is a safe conclusion considering her remarks as she continues: "However, even honesty had its limits. Proud as we were of our business ethics, we both [she and her partner] knew that this wasn't the sort of enterprise we wanted to operate under our own names." One wonders, why not? The answer appears in her valedictory remarks on prostitution toward the end of the book:

> Like their counterparts in the other helping professions, our girls brought tenderness and comfort into our clients' lives. We were *there* for them. We listened to them. We made them feel better. We gave to them emotionally, and we gave to them physically. Sex may be its own reward, but touching and hugging are the most healing and life-enhancing activities in the world.

> Our society still needs to learn to tolerate the idea of women making a living by being intimate with men. Some people say that prostitution is degrading. Certainly it can be, but not in the agency I operated. I can think of a lot of jobs that are considerably more degrading than sharing an enjoyable evening with an attractive, successful man who is delighted to have you there and is willing to pay top dollar for your company.

> But because prostitution is still illegal, the management side has attracted some fairly disgusting people.[5]

If only prostitution were not illegal, the reasoning goes, then people of class could get together for a fee, of course, and enjoy one another's company. Even though the relationship is brought about for money, we are to believe the intimacy for sale is just as "sincere" as that between people who share intimacy for reasons other than money. In an age of feigned "concern" for one another, this might be convincing to many people.

Why, indeed, deny the need busy important men on the move have for female companionship? Admitting how things really are is surely more honest than propping up antiquated moral ideas by means of vice laws. Only five percent of the sexual encounters portrayed on daytime television are between husband and wife. Who is watching these, anyway? It isn't as if the wives of these men wouldn't know what is happening, and it isn't as if they don't assuage their own loneliness, when their important husbands are on the move, through similar means. And it isn't as if there aren't busy important women on the move with the need for male companionship. But how does this peculiar logic work that in the name of honesty we discard the traditional and strongly held view that prostitution is morally wrong?

Again, it is by looking "objectively" or from the moral point of view too narrowly at the subject of sexuality. Once we look at the individual as a mere psycho-biological organism, we can see only the needs of the individual and none of the requirements of the relationships essential to the society the individual enjoys. Then, of course, some sex, even if it is purchased, is better than no sex because it is a source of pleasure and, if that's so, should be obtained through whatever techniques can best provide that pleasure. It is physically and psychologically healthful to do so, just as the Mayflower Madam says. We can even say that in her meticulous business matters she, her call girls, and their clients behaved "responsibly." And just as she says, it was more than mere sex. It was a relationship of "caring," if just for the evening. Those who call it "selling yourself" forget how many ways we sell ourselves in society today.

In contrast, the traditional moral interpretation of sexuality has been relational. Sex is more than a body function to be performed. Mere body function or not, the clients had to pay for it. This is okay according to the Mayflower Madam because it is a service. It's just that men don't like to admit they do pay for it. Why not? It's because we all know that with enough money in this society, at least, you can get what you want. But men typically want to think the women who give themselves to them do so because of them and not the money. And that goes to the heart of the matter. A man may need the sex, may just need a female companion, and will pay for it, but a man also needs to be acknowledged and loved for who he is. Some men even try to pay for that by having sycophants around telling them how great they are.

Somehow that's not enough. It's not enough because social life is not a matter of merely serving body functions. It is a matter of seeing how much we can accomplish by living together in orderly ways. We make sex a part of that order—family life, fidelity between man and woman through marriage, and procreation because we think that promotes greater value for us. Those who try to buy and sell that undermine this social purpose, if only because they confuse and rationalize sexuality into something other than what the society is trying to make of it. If there is hypocrisy involved, it is on the part of those who would be "on call" for three nights a week only so they could have a social life of their own, and on the part of those who wouldn't want their names to be public because it might cause social embarrassment.

Being morally literate is remembering the social nature of morality. In an era of the cult of individual freedom it is not surprising that the degree of moral illiteracy should be so high. We are trained to think self and self-satisfaction in all things. Morally speaking, there is absolutely nothing wrong with that. Moral illiteracy appears only where the quest for self-satisfaction turns into the delusion of self-sufficiency.

Notes

1. "Abe Lincoln in Illinois" by Robert E. Sherwood. Copyright © 1937, 1939 by Robert E. Sherwood. Copyright © 1965, 1966 by Madeline H. Sherwood. Reprinted by permission of Brandt & Brandt Literary Agents, Inc.
2. An excellent discussion of conscience occurs in Jonathan Bennett, "The Conscience of Huckleberry Finn," *Philosophy*, 49 (April 1974).
3. Sidney Biddle Barrows, *Mayflower Madam: The Secret Life of Sidney Biddle Barrows*, written with William Monk, New York, Arbor House, 1986.
4. *Ibid*
5. *Ibid*

Epilogue

୫ଠାଠୡ

Correcting for Drift

It is time to look again at the question, Who needs ethics? In Chapter I an adventure of James Bond was the departure point in search for an answer. Two heroic figures, 006 and 007, are on a mission to accomplish a purpose. Two must work together to get it done. Very little is spoken, no mention of rules, or codes, or values. The two know what they have to do and rely on each other to get it done. They can do it only with great risk of either or both lives. They are in a relationship of profound mutual dependence. The last thing in the world either of them needs is to suspect one will deceive, mislead, deliberately injure or otherwise betray the other. They must trust each other completely. Their lives depend on it.

This is a microcosm of morality. Anything else, whatever it may be, is not morality. If we have to keep one eye over our shoulder, hire police to guard us from each other, if we cannot rely on the candor of one another, if we cannot be sure we will share what we know for the protection of our lives, then we are not being ethical, whatever else we may be doing. So, when 006 does betray Bond, he could have done nothing worse, nothing more profoundly immoral. Everything was on the line. There was no room for disputation, deliberation, and debate. The fundamental ethical relation was breached, pure and simple. It is more than film entertainment when Bond calls 006 on that betrayal. Bond trusted, 006 calls trust a "quaint" idea, and we who are trying to live moral lives in today's world know just what 006 means.

Then the subject enlarges as the two secret agents talk of loyalty which, when shared by a people makes a society. Bond is the modern day Ulysses of his people, a hero. In mythology and legend a hero is a person of great strength admired for courage and nobility in exploits, especially in time of war. The hero is our ideal. Why not? The hero protects us, leads us with strength to do for us what we cannot do for ourselves. The hero advances our society protecting us from our enemies, foreign and domestic, dread diseases, famines, ignorance, and in all other ways pushing back the darkness.

Our heroes are many and varied, from Ulysses to John Glenn, Archimedes to Einstein, Hypocrites to Salk. James Bond may pale as a shallow modern fictional hero compared to Ulysses, but for our age of technology he is just as magical. Even when heroes go down in defeat, we are grateful to them for their sense of duty to act for our security and advancement. We see in them writ large the duty we each in our own small way have to one another. We also see the conflict between duty and desire. No hero just goes out and does things: he triumphs over adversity, obstacles so great they cause paralysis of fear in ordinary mortals. Bond must fulfill his duty to England before he fulfills his own desires with Natasha, service to nation over self, control of one's desires. We, too, cannot expect our society to continue providing for us unless we do what our society requires of us to keep it going, and that sometimes means limiting our individual desires.

Heroes of every people triumph over their adversities or go down nobly in defeat. Their cause is always just, because it is in service of the nation. People of all nations understand this, and that is one reason to expect people of different nations can eventually make common cause. Depth understanding of what makes morality in a people also yields understanding that can eventually lead to universally shared values and common approaches to securing them.

The moral authority we seek lies in the life we make together. It speaks to us when we ask how we should live and act together to optimize the life we share and assure its continuity for the benefits it affords. This is what we do when we try to discover if our action is right or wrong. This is how we find the higher value we know lies beyond merely pursuing our own ends and expecting others to do the same for themselves without regard to others. It is what assures our prosperity. This is how we push back the darkness and advance our civilization. It is the only way we can.

Doing what is right comes from respecting the life we make together. It is not always easy to know how to do this, and so we find it hard to be moral. This is in addition to the difficulty we have doing our duty over satisfying ourselves even when we know what we ought to do. That is also why being ethical requires judgment. It takes both training and experience, and there are no pat answers. So we have to take seriously the patterns of behavior expected of us in our society and depart from them only at our peril. When we do depart, we have to be guided by what furthers our common interest; otherwise, we sail off course and into the shoals of self-satisfaction without help of rescue.

Being moral is relying on the charts drawn by the collective experience of one's entire society. Morality is found in one's society. The ethicist's dream of discovering a universal rational or a factual foundation for morality remains just a dream. The difference between right and wrong cannot be reduced to a formula or a set of facts. It cannot be condensed from thin air. It has to be wrought on the anvil of the actual life of a people trying to be a society. Morality apart from life exists only in books.

Some will fear this conclusion because they see it as ethnocentrism, as society or culture dependent, and this way relativism or even subjectivism lies. Are we to conclude that ethics devolves into local beliefs and practices? Contact with other cultures shows us there are some practices all societies worthy of the name have in common. The experience of humans living together anywhere on this planet makes the struggle for survival and quest for fulfillment practically the same for everyone with the result that in the various societies throughout the world many practices for community living are similar. As contact among cultures continues to grow, these comparable rules provide a means of cross cultural moral understanding.

We can and do move from culturally shaped conventional moral wisdom to what appear to be general principles of living, such as "human rights," notions that we view as universal ethical precepts. But these, too, depend for their existence on common interest. As we find common interest in trade and other forms of mutual support, a purpose becomes shared and our ethical relationships grow. The trust we show each other in our society we extend to those in other societies. Why not? If we have reason to be ladies and gentlemen at home, we have also abroad in the measure we are treated in a corresponding manner we can understand by those we encounter outside our immediate society.

The same applies within the diverse and morally disintegrated nations we inhabit at the beginning of the Twenty-first Century. People with deep moral convictions believe we ought to be moral, and we imperil ourselves and others when we abandon the discipline of moral behavior. They ask, What can we do in this stormy sea of selfish disregard for others, narrow partisanship, and abstruse sophistry? The roar is so loud we cannot hear one another, and we seem to have stopped listening.

We can begin by finding those who understand the difference between right and wrong. Together we can affirm our trust for one another engendered by our mutual reliance. We can acknowledge that we do need one another and are responsible to one another. We can make it our business to notice matters of right and wrong in our public experience and keep before us our sense of morality and cultivate it as people have done throughout the ages. We do not have to bow to the criticism of "being judgmental." We do not have to live in a world without judgment. We can call actions performed in our midst right or wrong as long as our judgments are based on whether actions add or detract from shared purpose, what anchors morality into reality.

In 1727 Benjamin Franklin began a society known as the Junto for members interested in getting ahead in life and doing good and the relationship of these two. Franklin wrote "standing Queries" for the Friday evening meetings.[1] In one set of 24 he included the following:

6. Do you know of any fellow citizen, who has lately done a worthy action, deserving praise and imitation? or who has committed an error proper for us to be warned against and avoid?
7. What unhappy effects of intemperance have you lately observed or heard? of imprudence? of passion? or any other vice or folly?
8. What happy effects of temperance? of prudence? of moderation? or any other virtue?

Ben Franklin was taking right and wrong conduct seriously. We still can in our own time.

We do not have to return to the Eighteenth Century. When we see conduct we recognize as hazardous or destructive of our common life and goals together, we can examine and criticize it in moral terms to see what we, as a people, should have done to have prevented it, who specifically is responsible for it, and what is our proper response to it. We should do this instead of letting the news media direct our reflections into topics they can report on easily such as what are the schools doing about it and what government program do we need to solve our problem for us. We should also avoid leaping upon explanations couched in the seemingly scientific terms of psychology and sociology. When we do that, we deprive ourselves of the force of moral responsibility upon ourselves and those we have permitted to do antisocial acts.

When, for example, we have another school shooting, we must first ask who is responsible for it, so we can influence our people to be accountable for their behavior. Individuals who lack awareness of the mutual need and dependence we have for one another, our sense of moral responsibility to one another, are individuals to whom we appear meaningless things they can randomly diminish or destroy. In addition to who did the shooting, we must ask about those who knew the shooter, were relatives and friends, and why they did not help to avert the shooting.

We can focus on morality and moral responsibility with our friends, and get new friends who are interested. We can form clubs like Franklin's Junto. In fact, we already have clubs where morality should be important. We need to bring morality to the club agendas. There will be embarrassing moments when we do. We may appear naive. We may have to talk about things we have come to consider better handled by some agency or professional. But we are getting good at dealing with embarrassment in modern times. Law suits and media have solved that for us. Moral questions need to be raised publicly, and their answers sought.

Then those of us who are religious must recognize that our communities of faith are not coextensive with our society. No longer are we who make a life together all of one faith. So in our quest for moral recovery our religions can be our companions, but not our guides. Not until the society espouses any one of them, or the religious people of the society find a way to lead jointly toward common purpose, can religion be our moral authority. Each religion has vast stores of knowledge about human purpose and can raise expectations for us in ways we cannot do for ourselves. Religions can help us discover what we are, who we are, and what we can become. But people from the different religions have to learn to work together before undertaking to shape our social purpose and how we can achieve it together.

Next, we recognize that while law can help secure morality, law is not the same as morality. And while government can further our moral aims, government is not morality either. We have to stop acting as if our morality begins and ends with either or both law or government. Otherwise, we lose our ability to discern whether and when either is working in furtherance of morality.

Next, we have to understand who is in our society and who is not. We do this by discovering to whom we are responsible and to whom not, and who is responsible to us and who is not. Unless we do, there is no way we can expect moral behavior of anyone, not even ourselves. If, for example, we limit our relationships to securing rights for ourselves and others, most of what we have known as morality will devolve to arms length relationships. We will consider ourselves morally responsible only among family and close friends. That makes for an extremely small society for each of us, and it does not fully contemplate the reality and extent of our dependence on others. This will not happen if we insist on moral literacy, for ourselves and for others. It requires moral training for the young, but it begins with the promotion of moral awareness among adults.

Finally, there is something to say to those morally concerned who have felt isolated. "I know its wrong for business executives or government officials, for everyone, to lie, cheat, and steal, but what can I do?" Believe that there is a meaningful difference between right and wrong and act accordingly, and expect those with whom you live and work and those who are in positions of public responsibility to do likewise.

Note

1. L. Jesse Lemisch (ed.), *Benjamin Franklin: The Autobiography and Other Writings,* New York, New American Library, 1961, p. 199.

Index